BEYOND THE BLUE

A Survival Guide
for the Male Labeled,
and a Healthier Society for All

Chris Warren-Dickins LLB MA LPC

Zero Labels LLC
Publishing

Praise for *Beyond the Blue*

"*Beyond the Blue* is a thoughtful pathway to healthy living. Chris well understands that modern life is difficult and offers sound research from neuroscience, psychotherapy, and his professional experience. *Beyond the Blue* is accessible, 'achievable' and sensible, and well researched. It's a welcome reference for any and every person who is 'male labeled.'"

- The Honorable James E. McGreevey
Governor of New Jersey 2002 - 2004

"Stigma, societal beliefs, label-based expectations and no clear road map to care are real and pressing issues. *Beyond the Blue* peals back these obstacles and provides a user friendly 'survival guide' to self-care in a complicated world and meaningful clinical advice about seeking professional care. Don't just survive, choose to thrive. *Beyond the Blue* can help with that journey."

- David J. Griffith, MS, CCS, LCADC
President & C.E.O., Vantage Health System

"*Beyond the Blue* is **packed** with tools to 'survive and thrive.' Chris Warren-Dickins provides essential psychoeducation accompanied by awareness and solution-based exercises that are sure to benefit any willing reader. The author's personal passion to offer help to the male labeled is unquestionable."

- Jill Fellner, MSW, LCSW

"Chris Warren-Dickins's survival guide is not only for the male labeled but is also a resource for anyone challenged by abuse, anxiety and depression. Packed with fresh new metaphors and time-tested exercises this book speaks knowingly to a whole spectrum of human experiences and identities. *Beyond the Blue* is a timely addition to self-help and professional references."

- Suzanne Saldarini, MA, LPC, NCPsyA

Disclaimer: The contents of this book are for informational and supportive purposes only and are not intended to replace the services of a mental health or medical professional. Should you have any questions about the material set out in this book, contact your clinician or doctor. If you need immediate help and you are in crisis, seek immediate, professional help. Here are your options: Call 911 (if it is available in your area), take yourself to the Emergency Room of your nearest hospital, call a friend or family member, and ask them to take you to the nearest Emergency Room, call the National Suicide Helpline on 800-273-8255 / www.suicidepreventionlifeline.org

Beyond the Blue
A Survival Guide for the Male Labeled, and a Healthier Society for All

Print ISBN: 979-8-9851024-1-3 (Hardback)
Print ISBN: 979-8-9851024-0-6 (Paperback)
Ebook ASIN: B09HJNNS2Q

Printed in the United States of America
First printing edition 2021
Published by Zero Labels LLC

Cover design by Emily Mahon
Images in cover photo used under license from Shutterstock.com
Editing by Susan Schader
Headshot photo of Chris Warren-Dickins by Jean Terman Photography

Dedication

This Survival Guide is dedicated to the patience and support of my husband, Mikey, and our two children, Lucille and Willow.

In memory of my "Uncle" Gavin John Warren, who never got Beyond the Blue of their male label.

Chris Warren-Dickins LLB MA LPC

Table of Contents

INTRODUCTION

As a psychotherapist, I love to help all sorts of people with all sorts of problems. And in the hope of a safer, healthier society for all, I aim to provide mental healthcare to the people who are least likely to access it – thus the inspiration for this *Survival Guide*, which will help in getting *beyond the blue of the male label*. The rates of suicide and trauma are the highest amongst the *male labeled*, yet they are the least likely to access mental healthcare. This is even more significant when the male label intersects with a person's racial or ethnic identity, their true gender identity, and their sexuality. Untreated depression, anxiety, relationship conflict and anger, and trauma pose a risk for all of us in society.

I work a great deal on the following areas: Eye movement desensitization and reprocessing therapy (EMDR) (an approach commonly used for trauma), Affirmative LGBTQ+ therapy, and *"Men's therapy"* (in other words, how to survive the male label). I have professional and personal experience of all three areas, as I am a survivor of trauma, I am queer, I was assigned the male label at birth, and I am non-binary. However, there are limitations with my perspective given my privilege as someone who is White, Finnish-born, British-raised, living on the East Coast of the United States, and a college educated professional (to name just a handful of examples of my privilege).

Who are the male labeled?

Male labeled refers to anyone who was assigned the male sex label at birth. I chose the term "male labeled" instead of "assigned male at birth" because I wanted to emphasize that labels (whether a sex label, diagnostic, or any other label) often blind us to the opportunities to survive and thrive, despite depression, anxiety, relationship conflict, and trauma.

Society uses the male sex label to form assumptions about how people should act and feel, and these pose significant obstacles to adequate mental healthcare. One of the greatest obstacles is to assume that the male labeled is one homogenous group, and so I have written this Survival Guide to address these obstacles, acknowledging that the male labeled comprises people of all gender identities (including cisgender, transgender, non-binary, gender queer, two spirit, bigender, and gender diverse), of all sexualities (including bisexual, heterosexual, gay, queer, or pansexual), and of all racial or ethnic identities.

I am here to support you, not to create dependence

I have always struggled with the concept of an "expert." I rebelled against any ordained minister who told me how I should or should not live my life, and when I first trained and qualified as a lawyer, I winced at the concept of clients looking "up" to me. It was even more painful when I witnessed some of my colleagues believing the hype and puffing themselves up with self-importance like strutting peacocks.

When I decided to leave the legal profession and retrain as a psychotherapist, I found a similar issue with the way some people viewed therapists. Clients would look to me as some sort of oracle, clinging to my every word as if I could somehow solve all their problems. And I had colleagues who believed in such hype. They would dance around client issues, throwing this technique and that, and it would often turn out to be a load of smoke and mirrors (for a very high price).

When it came to writing this Survival Guide, I feared it might perpetuate the same type of hype. So let's get one thing clear: There is no such thing as a miracle cure for depression, anxiety, relationship conflict, and trauma. Instead, this Survival Guide is a chance for you to gain insight into the *Survival Tools* you already possess. In the rush and hustle of daily life, we rarely get a chance to stop and really look at our own process; working through the Guide provides a valuable opportunity to do so.

In this Survival Guide, I offer theories that may or may not resonate with you, and I point out a few blind spots you might have missed. But do not come to rely on this Survival Guide any more than you should rely on your therapist. Lean into the guidance I offer, but don't depend on it, because you will reach the end of the Survival Guide and, as you step away from the support it offers, you will need to support yourself. And this will be possible because the ultimate arbitrator in all of this, the true expert, is you.

As you make your way through this Survival Guide, you may find that my own use of labels does not quite reflect your own experience, or even inadvertently offends you by failing to be inclusive. I have made every effort to avoid this, but if this happens, please let me know via the contact page on my website, www.chriswarrendickins.com

CHAPTER 1

WHY SO BLUE?

Blue is the color that represents the male sex label, but it is also the color of melancholy, depression, and the ice-blue chill of death. One sometimes leads to the other, as it did late one night on a forest track in the woods at Braeside of Lethen, Nairn, Scotland. Their name was Gavin Warren, the year was 1988, and my "uncle" was 32 years old when they died by suicide.

During the short journey that was Gavin's life, they stumbled over life's challenges, unable to navigate their thoughts or emotions because Gavin was blinded by the male label that had been slapped over their eyes at birth. Gavin had been taught that "Big boys don't cry," and they should focus on their education and career, instead of talking about their feelings or needs.

When Gavin experienced trauma, the male label blinded them to the signs that they needed help, and so the *Beast of Depression* started to close in. By the time they recognized this Beast, for all its crushing weight of hopelessness, Gavin had strayed too far from the beaten path, and was teetering on the edge of an abyss.

Before Gavin died, they reached out for help, but they were unable to communicate in a way the healthcare professionals could understand. All they saw was Gavin's "angry silence," instead of the distress that lay within, and so these professionals sent Gavin on their way and to the woods at Braeside of Lethen.

Why Do You Need a Survival Guide?

Life's journey is a wilderness. If statistics are to be believed, at some point during life's journey, you are likely to encounter one or more of the following threats to your well-being:

- Depression snarling over your shoulder like a beast
- Anxiety burning through the pit of your stomach like a fireball
- Conflict with the people in your life, the companions accompanying you as you travel through life's wilderness
- Ten tons of trauma crushing down on you.

So you need to be prepared. These potential pitfalls could threaten your career, a business you have spent years building up, your education, the relationship you have with your partner, friends, and family, or the well-being of the children you have created.

Although these threats might seem inevitable, the attendant suffering and loss are far from inevitable. Using the latest research in neuroscience, research from the most effective approaches to psychotherapy, and my years of experience as a psychotherapist, I have put together a Survival Guide to help you live to your full potential, to not only survive, but to thrive in that wilderness.

True Survival Goes Beyond the Blue of the Male Label

If we are truly going to survive and thrive, despite depression, anxiety, relationship conflict, or trauma, everyone needs to see beyond the blue of the male label. A male label is a one-moment categorization to allocate a sex label, and it will have an impact on how you are conditioned, and how others view you, but it does not tell us the whole story. You are not simply the *male labeled*.

To truly know how to survive and thrive, despite depression, anxiety, relationship conflict, and trauma, we need to look beyond the blue of the male sex label, and consider how this label intersects with

- your true gender identity – you might be cisgender, transgender, non-binary, or gender queer;
- your sexuality – you might be bisexual, gay, heterosexual, queer, or pansexual;
- your racial or ethnic identity;
- your religion, immigration status, socioeconomic status, and your level of education.

These components to your identity, and your experiences of how they intersect with the male label, are crucial if we are to understand the full extent of your depression, anxiety, relationship conflict, and trauma. For example:

- Your access to mental healthcare might be undermined by structural inequality.
- The adequacy of the help you get might be impacted by racism, transphobia, biphobia, homophobia, or any other sort of discrimination by the diagnosing healthcare professional.
- You might live with the additional weight of *marginalized stress* and *microaggressions* as a result of societal privilege.

We will explore more of this in Chapter 5 and Chapter 6.

In a Patriarchal Society, Why Help the Male Labeled?

In a patriarchal society such as the United States, the male label is associated with assumed power and privilege. So why help the male labeled?

First, because the male labeled are less likely to seek help for emotional distress, and mental healthcare becomes even less accessible when we consider aspects of a person's identity including, for example, racial or ethnic identity, true gender identity, or sexuality.

If the male labeled are not going to access mental healthcare at a professional's office, it is my job to provide it in any way I can. No book is going to act as a substitute for psychotherapy, but if I were to carry out a cost-benefit analysis, it is better to offer help in the form of a Survival Guide than to provide no help at all.

Second, any person's untreated depression, anxiety, relationship conflict, and trauma has the potential to harm the whole of society. There are already numerous self-help books for the female labeled, but there are none for the male labeled that

- base the guidance on the latest research in neuroscience, research from the most effective approaches to psychotherapy, and years of experience from a trained and experienced psychotherapist;
- consider the intersection of the male label with aspects of your identity (for example, your racial or ethnic identity, sexuality, or true gender identity);
- consider the unique challenges and strengths that arise as a result of the male label, and the people who live with the male labeled;
- take you beyond the blue of the male label, viewing you beyond the overly simplistic binary opposite to the female labeled;
- paint a more realistic picture of the multiple shades of the male label, acknowledging that it is as arbitrary as the color blue, as overly simplistic as the term "toxic," and as restrictive as a blindfold.

Third, it is far too simplistic to assume power and privilege based on a binary choice of a male sex label or a female sex label. Here are some reasons:

- The power and privilege associated with the male label is assumed. The reality is far more complicated. For example, does a female-labeled, college-educated director of a Fortune 500 company who is cisgender and heterosexual have less power and privilege than a male-labeled person who is uneducated, unemployed, non-binary, and gay?
- There are more survivors of sexual violence amongst the female labeled but there are more victims of suicide and survivors of trauma amongst the male labeled. This comparison is also overly simplistic because the statistics vary dramatically if you look beyond the male or female sex label, and compare the statistics for sexual violence, suicide, and trauma amongst people of
  - different racial or ethnic groups;
  - different gender identities; and
  - different sexualities.

If we are truly to survive and thrive, despite the threats of depression, anxiety, relationship conflict, and trauma, and if there is going to be less harm for the whole of society, we need to look beyond the blue of the male label.

This Survival Guide will strike a balance between

- not being blinded by the male label, and only seeing a person in terms of this label; and
- maintaining awareness that depression, anxiety, relationship conflict, and trauma need to be seen from a societal, and not just an individual, perspective. There are structural issues that impact these mental health issues, the male label, and

8

how it intersects with aspects of a person's identity, including their racial or ethnic identity, true gender identity, and sexuality.

This Survival Guide will also strike a balance between the realities that

- we have agency over certain aspects of our lives, so there are self-help tips we can use to alleviate *some* of the harm associated with the male label; but also
- there is a limit to this. We are limited by the environment in which we live, whether our relationships, both intimate and wider, or societal structures. We can try to change ourselves, and try to change our relationships or societal structures, but others must change as well.

What Lies Ahead for You

Like blazes on a trail, I will guide you through the rougher paths of the journey that is your life. Whether it is depression, anxiety, relationship conflict, or trauma, you need to know how to prepare for these darker days, what to do when the storm arrives, and how to prevent yourself from getting blown over the cliff's edge, plunging you from disturbance to crisis.

The good news is that you are already carrying essential Survival Tools, as we will see below. I will just teach you how to use these tools effectively and efficiently.

In this Survival Guide you will find the following chapters:

- Beyond the Blue of your Depression (Chapter 2)
- Beyond the Blue of your Anxiety (Chapter 3)
- Beyond the Blue of your Relationship Conflict and Anger (Chapter 4)

- Beyond the Blue of your Trauma (Chapter 5)
- Beyond the Blue of Bad and Ugly Help (Chapter 6)

You can choose to jump to a chapter that grabs your attention, or you can read the Survival Guide chronologically. Either way, you will get the same benefits:

- You will learn how to spot the issue (depression, anxiety, relationship conflict and anger, or trauma).
- You will reflect on your understanding of the unique challenges and strengths that arise from the male label, and how it impacts depression, anxiety, relationship conflict and anger, and trauma. In Chapters 5 and 6, you will also reflect on how the male label intersects with aspects of your identity, including your racial or ethnic identity, your true gender identity, and your sexuality. For example, we will explore marginalized stress and microaggressions that result from societal privilege.
- You will learn how to use your backpack of Survival Tools to increase your chances of surviving and thriving, despite the potential harm from depression, anxiety, relationship conflict, and trauma.
- You will learn how to construct and maintain a *Shelter of Resilience* to reduce the impact of depression, anxiety, relationship conflict and anger, and trauma.

Mental Workout Routines

Included throughout this Survival Guide are *Mental Workout Routines* for you to complete. I can already hear the groans, as if I am a fifth-grade teacher assigning something during the last week before summer. I get it, we all have busy lives, and you just want to know the answers without having to jump through extra hoops as if you were an acrobat in a traveling circus.

But if you truly want to get beyond the blue of the male label, and improve your life, if you want to stop doing things that threaten the peace and stability of your home life, if you want to stop avoiding that next step in your business, complete the Mental Workout Routines. And besides, studies have shown that writing things down can really help to concretize your learning.

Still not buying it? Okay, how about I incentivize you. If you score more than 50 bonus points in the Mental Workout Routines in this Survival Guide, I will reward you with additional bonus material. More of that when you get to the end of our journey together.

Help Beyond the Labels

Throughout this Survival Guide, I will offer an alternative approach to the "corner-cut logic" that is labeling. When it comes to survival of depression, anxiety, relationship conflict, or trauma, labels can sometimes fail to help because you are more complex and sophisticated than that. And as we will see, the male sex label can blind us to the reality that the male labeled are capable of experiencing emotional distress and vulnerability as a result of depression, anxiety, relationship conflict, and trauma.

Labels are also value-laden, and we can see from history how they have been used to objectify and control others. For example, until as recently as 1973, the American Psychological Association labeled homosexuality as a "mental illness."

Labels offer a false sense of hope for some who find uncertainty anxiety provoking. Some believe that if they can label someone, they can predict their behavior, thoughts, and even emotions. But when it comes to human behavior, human thoughts, and human emotion, labels can be misleading and inexact.

Throughout this Survival Guide, we will avoid the oversimplification of diagnostic labels. The dividing line between one diagnosis and another, or even one diagnosis and no diagnosis, relies on data that is far from exact, and sometimes a diagnosis is used to objectify someone, at best, and pathologize them, at worst. I have heard colleagues dismissively refer to their clients as "problematic borderlines," "bipolars," or "narcissists" without any attempt to understand them.

Sometimes a healthcare professional will objectify someone in this way because that professional is attempting to manage their own anxiety about uncertainty. They cannot bear to leave things unknown, so they slap a label on their client. In the United States there is a higher rate of diagnosis of the male labeled when it comes to *externalizing disorders* such as attention-deficit disorder, oppositional defiant disorder, conduct disorder, antisocial personality disorder, or substance-related disorders. Some argue that these diagnoses are given to the male labeled at a higher rate because the male label blinds the diagnosing healthcare professionals to other potential diagnoses, such as depression, anxiety, and trauma.

The higher rate of diagnosis of these externalizing disorders is compounded when we consider parts of a person's identity beyond the blue of their male label. For example, some argue that racism, transphobia, biphobia, or homophobia on behalf of the diagnosing healthcare professional plays a part in the diagnosis of an externalizing disorder for:

- A person who is Black, Indigenous, or a Person of Color;

- A person who is transgender, non-binary, gender queer, two spirit, bigender, gender diverse, or any other gender identity that is not cisgender;
- A person who is bisexual, gay, pansexual, asexual, queer, or any other sexuality that it is not heterosexual.

As we will see in Chapter 6, there may be reasons why you want your healthcare professional to give you a diagnosis (for example, to secure funding for your treatment), and your healthcare professional should discuss this openly with you, without any assumption that they hold the deciding vote.

Your Survival Tools

Later in this Survival Guide you will learn how to identify depression, anxiety, relationship conflict, and trauma, and you will also learn about the trail of destruction all this can leave.

But it isn't all gloom and doom, for your Survival Tools can help:

- Survival Tool #1: *Action Pack* — This is your behavior. Certain actions you take, or don't take, can make you less vulnerable to the potential harm from depression, anxiety, relationship conflict, and trauma.

- Survival Tool #2: *Head Gear* — This refers to your beliefs and assumptions. The way you think can make things better.

- Survival Tool #3 – *Flashlight* — This is your emotions, which you can use to communicate important information to yourself, and to others. You also have a *Dimmer Switch* on that Flashlight to regulate how

13

you feel; sometimes you need to turn it down, and sometimes you need to turn it up.

The only snag, however, is that when you feel vulnerable, you can end up misusing your Survival Tools and trapping yourself in a *vicious cycle*:

- Your Action Pack — The more vulnerable you feel, the less you do the things that once made you feel good.

- Your Head Gear — The less you do, the fewer positive experiences you have, and so you become more negative in your thinking. Trapped in inactivity, your Head Gear may start to develop faults; for example, you start to label yourself a "failure."

- Your Flashlight — Hastening into retreat, you dim the Flashlight of your emotions to a dull glow, as dark as the thoughts that were starting to circle. You *believe* you are a failure, so you *feel* like one, and you *do* less, and then you see yourself in a less positive light.

And so, the vicious cycle continues.

Figure 1 - The Vicious Cycle

But it doesn't have to be this way. The more familiar you are with your own Survival Tools, the easier it will be to use them to break free of this cycle.

*   *   *

Survival Tool #1 — Your Action Pack (Behavior)

Old, New, and Borrowed, to Get You Beyond the Blue

The first of your Survival Tools is your Action Pack. You can engage in actions that once made you feel good (the "old"), or you can create new experiences from your own brainstorming (the "new"), or from ideas that are borrowed from others (the "borrowed").

The Old

If you dig deep inside your backpack, you will find a whole range of actions you have engaged in the past — actions that made you feel better. You need to try these actions again.

- Do you remember a fist pump in the air when you crossed the finish line in a race?
- What about that glow when you were congratulated for going that extra mile at work?
- Can you recall the joy of laughter when you hung out with your mates?
- What about that sense of connection when your partner put their arm around you on the boardwalk?

Why reinvent the wheel? Dig deep and find experiences from the past that you can replicate in the present. The more you do what once made you feel good, the less negative your thoughts will be, thus uplifting and lightening your emotions.

The New, and Borrowed

Your Action Pack can be as exciting or mundane as you like (reading an engaging piece of fiction, or watching a Netflix series, for example), provided you include the creation of new experiences. Studies have shown that the more you are introduced to new experiences, the more dopamine, the feel-good chemical, is produced in the brain.

If you ever get stuck on a train with a neuroscientist, ask them about *neuroplasticity.* By engaging in new experiences, you are literally training your brain to create new neural pathways. Your new behavior will help create a new understanding of yourself, and the world around you.

Repetition and variety are key here, for it takes between three and six months to create new neural pathways, and it helps to engage as many parts of the brain as possible. For example, if your depression leaves you feeling dark and sluggish, use all five of your senses to visualize and engage in bright and energetic images and activities.

Lighten the Load of Your Action Pack

Later in this Survival Guide you will have a chance to identify the components to your own Action Pack. But you need to be selective, because you don't want to overload your backpack with an endless list of actions you never get around to.

You can lighten the weight of your Action Pack by disposing of any components that do not pass at least one of these three tests:

1. The Test of Mastery – Are the components to your Action Pack likely to help you develop a sense of mastery? Whether you choose to repeat something you have done in the past, or you try a new activity, will it give you a sense of accomplishment?

2. The Test of Opposite Attraction – Does the component to your Action Pack create an emotion that is opposite to what is evoked by your depression, anxiety, relationship conflict, or trauma? For example, if anger leaves you feeling out of control or powerless, engage in activity that establishes a sense of control or certainty (for example, playing golf).

Engaging in actions that evoke opposite emotions is one approach to breaking a vicious cycle. Another way is to mindfully accept, without judgment, the emotions you are currently experiencing. Sort of like surfing a wave, the idea is that if you experience the peak of an emotion and stay with it, you will then experience relief as it subsides. Accepting and experiencing emotions without judgment will help you develop more resilience, and a sense of mastery. We will explore this further when we look at the Flashlight Survival Tool.

3. The Test of Appreciation – Does the component to your Action Pack engage you in at least one activity that helps you to develop an appreciation for what you have? For example, if you volunteer at a homeless shelter, you will appreciate the home you rent or own. Or if you spend time with the silliness and disorganization of your kids, this might help you appreciate the more playful side of life in contrast to your structured and serious work life.

A SMART Action Pack

Once you identify the components to your Action Pack, you need to plan how and when you are going to use each component to ensure you are not trapped in the vicious cycle mentioned previously.

One tried and tested strategy is to use the SMART approach to evaluate each component of your Action Pack. First you identify **S**pecific actions to take, then you **M**easure them, and then determine how **A**chievable, **R**ealistic and **T**ime-bound they are.

S is for Specific – Looking at each component to your Action Pack, how specific are these planned activities? For example, you plan to hang out with a friend:
What actions are involved? Do you intend to hang out in-person, online, or over the phone?
If it is in-person, where are you going to hang out? At the beach? At someone's place? At the gym?

M is for Measurable – How many times do you plan to hang out with your friend? Just the once? Once a month? Once a week?
And for how long? A quick half hour catch-up? Or a whole evening? Or maybe a whole day?

A is for Achievable – If you are referring to a friend who lives in Florida, and it is an in-person meet-up, this is going to be hard if you live in New York.

R is for Realistic – Ah, realism, the flaw in every best-laid plan. You might have planned to hang out with a friend because you remember your college days together, when you could hang out with them every day. If you are now married and you have an endless supply of kids in every corner of your life, this is not going to be a realistic component to the Action Pack. Could you aim for a hangout once a month, or every other week, as a more realistic first step?

T is for Time-bound – When are you going to use each component to your Action Pack? You don't want to do it all at once, and risk burnout, but you also don't want to procrastinate, finding excuse after excuse to end up doing just as little as you have been already.

You can create a schedule along the following lines:

Component to your Action Pack	Time	Day, and frequency	Intensity
Facetime with your friend in Ohio	2pm, after the kids are done with their activities	Weekends only, once every two weeks	10 minutes minimum, 30 minutes maximum
Workout at the gym	7pm, when the kids are in bed	Mondays, Wednesdays, and Fridays	20 minutes minimum, 1 hour maximum
Etc. – you get the picture			

Figure 2 - How to make your Action Pack Time-bound

Later in this Survival Guide, you will have a chance to create your own schedule to ensure that your Action Pack is SMART.

Of the three Survival Tools, your Action Pack is the quickest and easiest way to break the vicious cycle. The trouble with the Action Pack, however, is

- it doesn't always work;
- it may only work for a short time;
- it may not get to the root of the problem;
- it may mask important information your emotions are trying to communicate to you.

This is why we also need the other Survival Tools to break the vicious cycle.

* * *

Survival Tool #2 – Your Head Gear (Your Thoughts)

Your Head Gear – your thoughts, beliefs, and assumptions about yourself, others, and the world around you – can help or hinder you when it comes to the impact of depression, anxiety, relationship conflict, and trauma. It really depends on what you do with this essential Survival Tool.

Figure 3 - The Vicious Cycle

This is not a new idea. Many psychotherapists (particularly those who use an approach called *cognitive behavioral therapy* (CBT)) believe that if we can become familiar with our Head Gear, we can identify the unhelpful or *faulty thoughts*, and change them. And if we change our thoughts, we can change how we feel, even if the circumstances cannot be changed.

On the one hand, this seems like a freeing concept. You might not be able to move to avoid the neighbor who drives you nuts, but if you adjust your faulty Head Gear, and challenge your beliefs and assumptions about that neighbor (in other words, if you adjust your thoughts), you may feel less vulnerable to the impact of depression, anxiety, relationship conflict, or trauma.

But it doesn't always work that way. There may be, for example, structural issues that are beyond your control, and no matter how much you challenge your thought process, the situation feels equally as dire. If that very same neighbor is racist, transphobic, biphobic, or homophobic, no amount of Head Gear adjustment will make a blind bit of difference. And to place all the onus on you, with an expectation that you and only you change, is not just irresponsible, it perpetuates the trauma inflicted by this structural abuse.

Nor is an adjustment of your Head Gear an attempt to achieve some sort of *Clockwork Orange* type dystopia where we clamp your eyes open and force ourselves to "Think happy thoughts, damn it!"

But if you develop an awareness of the usual faults that can develop in your Head Gear, you can take action to identify and fix those faults, and this might offer some sort of relief while we work towards, or wait for, structural reform.

As Simple as A-B-C

To use your Head Gear as a Survival Tool, you first need to become familiar with it. Just as you wouldn't lift the hood of an Aston Martin and start tinkering around if you know nothing about that engine, you cannot change anything about your Head Gear if you don't understand the patterns in your thoughts.

The trouble is, these patterns are formed rapidly every moment, without you even noticing it. Daily, you are consumed with the wilderness that is life's journey – when and where you might acquire your next meal, where to set up shelter, and why your travel companions are so flipping annoying – that you do not notice what's firing away in your Head Gear at any given moment.

A neglected piece of machinery will keep whirring away until the sparks start to fly, or it suddenly comes to a blank-minded stop. So, before that happens, let's get familiar with the finely tuned piece of machinery that is your Head Gear.

To do this, many psychotherapists use an ABC log to identify *beliefs* and *assumptions* (thoughts) about things that evoke a strong reaction in us. Whether it is a feeling of sadness, boredom, fear, anger, or shock:

> <u>You make assumptions</u> about how things should or should not be, or how you should have behaved or thought or felt in that moment.
> You also fill the gap where you are missing knowledge, assuming, for example, what someone thinks about you.
> <u>You also carry around beliefs</u> about yourself, others, and the world around you. For example, you might believe that "The world is unsafe," or "Others cannot be trusted," or "I am unlovable."

I have set out below an example of an ABC log. Familiarize yourself with it because we will continue to use it throughout this Survival Guide.

A	B	C	D	E
Activating Event	Beliefs & Assump-tions	Conse-quences	Dispute	Evaluate

Figure 4 - ABC Log

Let's look at each component to the ABC log, so you will be ready, in the chapters to come, to fill one out for yourself.

Column A – The Activating Event (or Trigger)

The *activating event* (or *trigger*) refers to what was happening at the time you were feeling particularly vulnerable (for example, when you felt particularly depressed, anxious, or angry).

- Were you working late at work?
- Did you just have an argument with your partner or best friend?
- Were you noticing you had not seen any of your family for quite some time?
- Were you hanging around with the work colleague who constantly berates you?

The focus here is more on what is happening, rather than any beliefs or assumptions you are making about your experience, which we'll explore later. Even though it might not seem important when you write it down, the more information you gather, the greater chance you have to identify a pattern.

For some people, the terms "activating event" and "trigger" may not be helpful because there is no specific moment when they suddenly notice their depression, anxiety, or anger. For some, their discontent lingers, leaving a foggy trail that leaves their life seeming distant and obscure. If this is the case for you, use column A of the ABC log to record noteworthy times when you felt particularly foggy, or particularly distant. For example, during those times, what was going on? Who was involved? Was there anything out of the ordinary about what you (or others) were doing?

Column B – Your Beliefs and Assumptions

At the time of the activating event, what were your beliefs or assumptions? As we saw above, these can make you more or less vulnerable to the impact of depression, anxiety, relationship conflict, or trauma, so it is important to examine them carefully. Only if we are clear about the beliefs or assumptions we are making, can we start to closely examine our Head Gear for faults.

For any belief you identify, rate the strength of your belief on a scale of 1 to 7, where
    1 = you don't really believe it, and
    7 = you wholeheartedly believe it.
This rating will serve as a baseline when we dispute and re-evaluate those beliefs in columns D and E of the ABC log.

Although numerical ratings can seem arbitrary, they do help give things a focus, and research indicates that when people see an improvement (even if that is only reflected numerically), this can help inspire further improvement in mood.

Later in this Survival Guide, we will examine seven common faults that can develop in our Head Gear and keep us trapped in a vicious cycle, leaving us more vulnerable to the impact of depression, anxiety, relationship conflict, and trauma.

Column C – Consequences (Emotional and Behavioral)

As a result of the activating event that you noted in column A of the ABC, and the beliefs and assumptions you noted in column B –

- **How do you feel?** (the *emotional consequences*)
  If you feel depressed, anxious, or angry, for example, how would you rate that distress on a scale of 0 to 10, where
  - 0 = not at all, and
  - 10 = extreme intensity.

- **What did you do (or not do)?** (the *behavioral consequences*)

Column D – Disputing or Correcting Faulty Beliefs and Assumptions

To use your Head Gear to break the vicious cycle, you need to fix any faults that can develop in your Head Gear. Later in this Survival Guide we will look at how you can do this, paying particular attention to depression, anxiety, relationship conflict, and trauma.

Column E – Evaluating Beliefs and Emotions

Once you fix the faults in your Head Gear, you can re-evaluate your beliefs and emotions.

Re-evaluate Your Beliefs
Remember that in column B of the ABC log, you identified initial beliefs and assumptions, and you rated each belief on a scale of 1 to 7?

Now you have fixed the faults in your Head Gear, how would you rate those initial beliefs now, on a scale of 1 to 7, where
> 1 = you don't really believe it, and
> 7 = you wholeheartedly believe it.

In column E of the ABC log, you might decide to create a new, more constructive belief to replace the above-mentioned (initial) belief. Try to give this new belief a rating from 1 to 7, where

1 = you don't really believe it, and
7 = you wholeheartedly believe it.

Re-evaluate Your Emotions
Remember that in column C you recorded the original score, on a scale of 0 to 10, for your depression, anxiety, or anger, for example?

Once you have used column D to fix the faults in your Head Gear, you need to rate your emotions (for example, your depression, anxiety, or anger) on a scale of 0 to 10, where
0 = A very low, flat-lined level of intensity, and
10 = An intense, mushroom-cloud level of intensity.

The theory is that you may see a decrease in this level of distress.

* * *

Your Head Gear, if used correctly and with any faults fixed, can be a most useful Survival Tool to reduce the potential harm of depression, anxiety, relationship conflict, and trauma. But your Head Gear and Action Pack are not the only Survival Tools. There is one final way to break the vicious cycle, and that is with the aid of your Flashlight.

* * *

Survival Tool #3 – Your Flashlight (Your Emotions)

You have a Flashlight, which is basically your emotions, and you can learn how to use this valuable tool to light your way out of the vicious cycle.

Your emotions communicate important information to yourself, and to others, and during dark and stormy nights,

the Flashlight may be the only thing that keeps you from
wandering over the cliff's edge.

Figure 5 - The Vicious Cycle

Why Carry a Flashlight?

As a psychotherapist, I find that so many of my clients
start off our work together by devaluing their emotions.
Here are some of the things they tell me:

"Emotions are a luxury I just don't have time for."
"Emotions are a commodity sold by spiritual hacks
who make a living out of dousing people in
aromatherapy oils and getting them to buy their Apps."
"Everyone is so obsessed with emotions, but that
won't help me to feed my kids or settle an argument
with my partner."
"Emotions are an inconvenience."
"If everyone lived by their emotions, the world would
be a chaotic and unsafe place."

Does any of this sound familiar?

The truth is, we need our emotions to survive. And not just to do that, our emotions can help us to thrive in business, at school, with our partners, our children, our friends, and our family.

If you are still not convinced, consider this:

- **Your emotions communicate important information to you.**
  Without your emotions screaming at you to get up and run from a roaming beast, you would end up devoured. Without your emotions alerting you there is danger, you would not have jumped up to stop your daughter from toppling out of the upstairs window.
  Your emotions are not some newfangled invention by someone who posts daily pictures of matcha tea on their Instagram profile. Emotions are hardwired into you to ensure and help you survive and thrive.

- **Your emotions motivate your behavior.**
  Emotions drive your behavior, giving you the energy to flee that stalking beast, and charging adrenalin around your body to reach your daughter just in time.
  In Chapter 5 we will take a closer look at this, but in brief, your sympathetic nervous system kicks in, and this activates the *fight-or-flight mode*. Fueled by adrenaline, your heart pumps faster, and your pupils dilate. This is all part of your natural survival (and thrive) system, and it kicks in without you having to buy an extra App. You don't even need any aromatherapy oils.

- **Your emotions communicate important information to others.**
  Without your emotions, how can you truly connect with others?
  How can you make love, share laughter, or warn others that they have crossed your boundaries?

- **Emotions are neither good nor bad.**
  They just exist, and no amount of denial or avoidance is going to change this. Let's make an important distinction here –

  Feeling an Emotion
  o Feeling an emotion is neither good nor bad. It just exists, whether or not you "should" feel this, given all the facts.
  o If you feel sad, angry, or lonely, this is neither good nor bad, and no one can tell you that you do not or should not feel that way.

  Acting on an Emotion
  o Whether or not you choose to act on an emotion might be good or bad, helpful or unhelpful.
  o If you choose to kick the cat because you are sad, or you punch a wall because you are angry, or you have an affair behind your partner's back because you feel lonely, how good or bad, or how helpful or unhelpful those actions are is up for debate, given all the facts.

Don't fall into the trap of thinking life is all about the Flashlight or using emotions to excuse poor behavior. You need a balanced use of all three of your Survival Tools — your Head Gear, Action Pack and Flashlight.

So you are now sold on the purpose of this Survival Tool, but if you want to break free of the vicious cycle, you need to know how to use it.

Let's take a closer look at the Flashlight's components.

Component 1
The Multicolored Words of the Flashlight

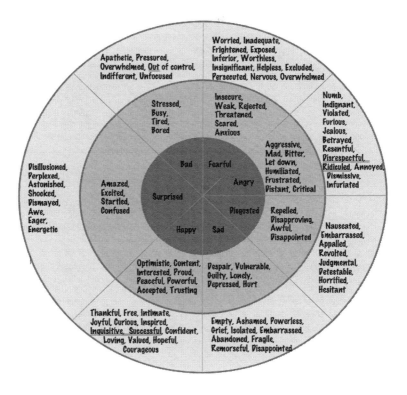

Figure 6 - The Full Spectrum of Your Emotions

When you are caught in the vicious cycle, you can get stuck if you are unable to communicate exactly how you feel. Sometimes the binary choice of "happy" or "sad" can be insufficient, and so you need to become familiar with the first component to the Flashlight: the full spectrum of the multicolored emotion words.

An ability to articulate the full palette of emotions gives you more choice when you need to communicate how you feel. This will, in turn, take you one step closer to understanding, and communicating, what you need. For example, you will be able to articulate that you need to feel safe, or that you need to be heard, or that things need to change, or stay the same.

You may not have heard of some of the shades of emotion words, perhaps because you were raised in a household where your caregivers only talked about the binary opposite of "happy" or "sad." So get an eyeful of this multicolored spectrum (Figure 6), and learn about each emotion.

But to name the emotion is only the half of it. You also need to identify the *intensity* of that emotion. For example, is that sadness a shrug of the shoulders, "bad stuff happens" kind of intensity, or a black hole of despair? How brightly is your Flashlight shining? In the previous section (when we were examining your Head Gear), we saw how you could rate the intensity of an emotion on a scale of 0 to 10, where:
    0 = A very low, flat-lined level of intensity, and
    10 = An intense, mushroom-cloud level of intensity.

Although numbers can sometimes seem artificial, they can help when you are tracking your progression through life's journey. For example, your depression, anxiety, relationship conflict and anger, or trauma might have evoked a level 8 despair last month, but you can see an improvement because you have not rated it higher than a 4 or 5 within the last few weeks.

The intensity of your emotions depends on a number of different sources of power, so let's review what powers this important Survival Tool.

Component 2 – The Power Pack in Your Flashlight

Your Flashlight needs fuel to power it, and so the intensity of your emotions will depend upon the amount of power you can get from the following sources:

- Sleep
- Food
- Drink
- Drugs, prescription or otherwise
- Exercise
- The absence of stressful experiences over a recent period.

The intensity of your emotions will also depend upon how much you have used the Flashlight in any given period. For example, you might have had a draining week of depressing setbacks, or you might have over-committed yourself to one too many events. As a result, your Flashlight might be reduced to the flicker of a barely visible glow.

Here are some examples that might intensify your emotions:

- You skip meals, leaving you feeling weaker and more tearful.
- You work too hard at work or at school, and you end up making mistakes.
- You stay up late at night, scrolling through TikTok, and you end up feeling hopeless and irritable the next morning.
- You drink too much alcohol or smoke too much weed at a party, knowing that you will sleep in too late the next morning, and end up cancelling plans.
- You skip your workouts and end up feeling sluggish and despondent.

- You fill your schedule with activities and end up cancelling half of them, leading to you withdrawing from your social circle out of shame and embarrassment.

Later in this Survival Guide, you will have a chance to identify your own patterns, so you can learn what powers, and what drains, your own Flashlight.

Component 3 – Master the Dimmer Switch

Although we should not ignore our emotions, there are times when their intensity makes our journey through the wilderness all the more difficult. We thus have to strike a balance between allowing our emotions in, but not to the extent that they leave us helpless and lost. You don't want the Flashlight to shine so brightly that it blinds you or your travel companions, so you need to learn how to master your Flashlight's Dimmer Switch.

The Dimmer Switch helps you to regulate your emotions by striking the following balance:

Sometimes you need to turn the intensity down – for example, you have been crying on and off for several hours, and now you need to go to work.

Sometimes you need to keep it at its current setting and use it to light your way.

Sometimes you need to turn it up – for example, you have felt flat and despondent, and now you need to feel the warmth of the sunshine on your face.

We are not looking for dramatic shifts, just a subtle increase or decrease in that emotion, depending on what might be best for you.

To master the Dimmer Switch and regulate your emotions, use any of the following techniques:

> grounding exercises
> breathing exercises
> visualization exercises

Each of these techniques offers an alternative, and a healthier, way to cope with your emotions. Much better than trying to distract yourself with excessive work, alcohol, drugs, excessive eating, or pounding your fist into the ground every night.

Later in this Survival Guide, I will guide you through some grounding, breathing, and visualization exercises to lessen the impact of depression, anxiety, relationship conflict, and trauma.

Surf the Light Waves of Each Emotion

As you saw from the previous section, sometimes you need to keep the Flashlight at its current setting and use it to light your way. You have already seen how valuable your emotions can be (for example, to communicate to yourself and others, and to motivate you), so you cannot keep avoiding them, distracting yourself from them, denying them, or trying to extinguish them (through excessive work, excessive food, or alcohol).

But the full intensity of an emotion can be scary. You might fear it will overwhelm or dominate you, and you just don't have the time to sit and cry or scream into your pillow every night.

The truth is that emotions are temporary and have
> a beginning (or a buildup);
> a middle (a peak); and
> an end (a subside).

I like to think of emotions as light waves that build up, peak, and then subside. You can see this in (Figure 7).

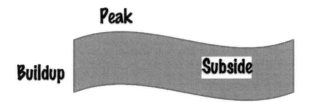

Figure 7 - How to Surf the Light Waves of Your Emotions

If you use a mindful approach to observe your emotions without trying to change them, if you stay with the emotions during the buildup and peak, you usually experience them subside. When you do this, you learn you have resilience, and you do not need to keep avoiding the emotion. This is called neuroplasticity, a process where your brain creates new neural pathways as a result of new experiences. By staying with the emotion, you teach your brain that this emotion is not some blinding light that will burn you to the core, and by staying with it, you can survive and thrive, in spite of the sadness or loneliness.

If you learn how to master the Dimmer Switch of your Flashlight, you are more likely to stay with the emotion. For example, with the help of a breathing exercise (as set out later in this Survival Guide), you can continue to feel the emotion, start to realize you have control over its intensity, and you can let a little more in. This gives you more confidence when it comes to surfing the next light wave of emotion for you have actual lived experience that you did not get overwhelmed by the intensity (or darkness) of that emotion. You emerged out the other side as the emotion started to subside.

* * *

Your Shelter of Resilience

Even with the aid of your Survival Tools, you cannot stay out in the wilderness forever. At some point you need to rest and recover your mental strength so you are more resilient in the face of depression, anxiety, relationship conflict, and trauma. To this end, you need to construct and maintain your *Shelter of Resilience* from four distinct walls of:

1. Self-Compassion
2. Self-Esteem
3. Self-Awareness through Acceptance
4. Self-Care.

Fear of Excessive *Selfing*

We have a gut-wrenching aversion to anything beginning with the word "self.*"* We fear that we will smack of narcissism, and we are embarrassed about the associations with self-love and self-interest. So when I suggest to my clients that they engage in a bit of self-compassion, self-awareness, or even good old-fashioned self-care, they dismiss it as indulgent navel-gazing. It is as if I suggested they follow a treatment plan of quinoa and avocado on toast while they run naked down the I-95.

When you board a plane, you are told to put on your oxygen mask before you help others. And yet there it is in all its glory: a shining example of pure, unadulterated *selfing.*

A healthy dose of selfing is strategic, sensible, and just plain common sense, because you cannot help others if you are dead. (Funny thing about oxygen: We can't live without it.). You don't want to see your travel companions drop dead around you while you happily gulp those delicious mouthfuls of oxygen, but you know that if you try to be the dumb hero, who happily helps others with their masks before you put on your own, you will end up the dead hero.

"'Ah," you might say, "but I am giving, and I am selfless. I don't need all those 'self' words" (except, apparently, selflessness, which seems to be one of the few "self" words that meets global approval). And that is all very well, so long as you don't need oxygen to survive.

Still not convinced? If you really are too proud to accept the help of self-compassion, self-esteem, self-awareness or self-care, think of your loved ones. As Helen Lovejoy implored in *The Simpsons,* "Won't someone please think of the children!" For their own survival, your kids might need a bit of selfing to construct their own Four Walls of a Shelter of Resilience. Monkey see, monkey do, and so those little monkeys are watching your every move. If you don't take sensible and strategic steps to ensure your survival, will they?

Wall One: Self-Compassion

During my years as a psychotherapist, I have helped the male labeled build and maintain their Shelter of Resilience, to reduce the impact of depression, anxiety, relationship conflict, and trauma. In all those years, the *Wall of Self-Compassion* has been the hardest to construct.

Too often what is erected is so lopsided that it quickly falls apart; the compassion they have for their children, partner, friends, or even work colleagues, stands tall and strong, like a towering brick wall of strength and support. And yet their self-compassion is small and paper-thin to the point of translucence.

What is self-compassion?

> You are kind to yourself.
> You see suffering and you want it to end.
> You know that we are all human, and so you recognize that mistakes can be made.
> You understand rather than criticize or punish.
> You adopt a mindful, balanced approach to life.

These are the hallmarks of compassion, and it can be applied to yourself as much as it can be applied to other people.

A titanium-strong Wall of Self-Compassion can be created by the same words you use with other people; kind words of understanding and acceptance that come so easily when you are referring to someone else but come so hard when you try to apply them to yourself.

Why do you find it easier to offer compassion to other people? You deserve as much understanding and acceptance as the next person. Find your strong, kind voice of self-compassion, and start to practice it today.

Self-Compassion Is in Our DNA

Clinical psychologist Professor Paul Gilbert claims that self-compassion is essential to maintain a well-balanced emotion regulation system. According to Gilbert, we have three emotion regulation systems:
- a "threat" system (for example, anger or criticism)
- a "drive" system (pursuit of achievement)
- a "soothe" system (calming, nurturing).

Our soothe system is activated when we receive compassion, including self-compassion. To maintain balance, all three systems are needed at different times:
- The threat system is required to keep us alert.

- The drive system is required to motivate us to achieve things.
- The soothe system is required to enable us to rest and digest. It also helps us to manage distress more efficiently.

Self-compassion is as natural as our fight-or-flight response. Self-compassion isn't just for wimps; it is a necessary tool for us to survive and thrive.

Get High on Self-Compassion

According to neuroscientists, self-compassion triggers the release of oxytocin, a hormone that produces a calming effect. Oxytocin has been linked to close connection, and it is released during sex, childbirth, and even when we play (with our pets, children, or we just become childlike and playful again).

So why wouldn't you want some more of this good stuff?

Cost-Benefit Analysis

If you really, *really* cannot let this compassionate voice in, carry out a cost-benefit analysis:

What is the cost of holding onto this belief that you, for some reason, don't deserve the same compassion you would offer to other people?

versus

What is the benefit of holding onto that belief?

When you carry out this analysis, make sure you include the true value of short-term *versus* long-term costs and benefits.

Delusions about Self-Compassion and Motivation

Some of you believe that self-compassion might quiet the voice of your harsh inner critic, making you a lazy no-getter.

Let's be clear. Constantly beating yourself up by criticizing yourself does not motivate you. In fact, studies say punishment will likely de-motivate you. It has long been established that positive reinforcement is the most effective way to motivate your children. So if positive reinforcement is more effective for your little monkeys, why are you not using self-compassion as a form of positive reinforcement for yourself? What is good for the goose is also good for the gander.

Later in this Survival Guide you will have a chance to assess the level of your own self-compassion. If you find that this essential wall to your Shelter of Resilience is a little weakened, fear not, because I have plenty of tips to help you reinforce it.

Wall Two: Self-Esteem

So far we have seen how to erect and maintain the first wall (self-compassion) of your Shelter of Resilience. But a one-walled shelter won't keep you safe from the threats posed by depression, anxiety, relationship conflict, and trauma. You also need a *Wall of Self-Esteem*.

Some of my clients have attempted to construct this wall using all sorts of unstable materials. I have seen a haphazard amalgam of sporting trophies, promotions at work, flashy cars, and even the square footage of their home.

To erect and maintain the Wall of Self-Esteem, you need to believe that you have worth regardless of anything you achieve or acquire. If your sense of self-esteem is conditional on any of the following things, then it is made of straw, and the Beast of Depression will huff and puff and blow it down with one fell swoop:

- advancement in your career
- a sizeable home
- an attractive partner
- a slim or muscular body
- a large bank account
- academic achievement
- more followers on social media
- any other form of higher social status.

These are all nice things to have, and they can be beneficial. But if your self-esteem *depends* on any of these, you need to reinforce it with something stronger – a sense of intrinsic value beyond anything that can be achieved from external sources.

Self-esteem is more than what you do; it is the value you place on yourself, and it goes to your core. It is an overall assessment of your worth, no matter what else happens in your life.

Signs of Low Self-Esteem

Low self-esteem is often revealed by excessive behavior; for example, someone might overwork, overeat, under-eat, and engage in excessive drinking or other substances. The list goes on.

You can also identify low self-esteem in the way a person interacts with their family or friends. For example:

- They consistently act aggressively or passively.
- They do not maintain appropriate boundaries with their friends and family.
- They are constantly anxious about pleasing others.

Other indicators of low self-esteem include:

- Labeling yourself a "loser," "stupid," a "loner," or any of the multitudes of ways you can make yourself feel awful.
- Assuming something bad happens because you are defective in some way (for example, you assume an argument with a colleague is your fault).
- Making your self-esteem contingent on achievement. You are of worth as a human being, regardless of what you achieve, so chill.
- Discounting your positives, such as saying to yourself:
  - *Nothing I say or do will ever be good enough,* or
  - *I may have been promoted three times in four years, but I didn't get promoted that one year,* or
  - *I was just lucky,* or
  - *Oh, it's nothing really,* when you have done something good or achieved something that is really quite great.
- You feel unable to do the things you need to in order to function; for example, you cannot bring yourself to eat, you cannot get out of bed, you cannot pursue that other career you have been longing for.
- You destroy relationships that would have been helpful or fulfilling.

Later in this Survival Guide, you will have a chance to rate your own self-esteem, and to strengthen your Wall of Self-Esteem.

Chris Warren-Dickins LLB MA LPC

Wall Three: Self-Awareness through Acceptance

With walls of self-compassion and self-esteem firmly in place, your Shelter of Resilience is starting to take shape. But with only two walls in place, you are still vulnerable to depression, anxiety, relationship conflict, and trauma. You also need to erect and maintain a *Wall of Self-Awareness* through *Acceptance*.

Throughout this Survival Guide you will have a chance to develop an awareness of
- your Action Pack (your behavior);
- your Head Gear (your thought process, including your beliefs and assumptions); and
- your Flashlight (your emotions).

However, no matter how self-aware you are, if there are matters outside of your control, you need to focus on developing a sense of acceptance. After all, there is always at least one annoying jackass at your gym who snorts phlegm and spits in the sink right next to you, or at least one megalomaniac senior executive at your place of work who claims credit for your every decision.

Acceptance does not mean we have given up and that we will forever remain like this. But if we have come up against a brick wall, it is more sensible to redirect our energy away from beating down that brick wall with our bare fists.

Here is a simple equation to explain how acceptance can help:

acceptance = emotional distress (you have accepted what you cannot change).

non-acceptance = emotional distress + further emotional distress (as a result of your non-acceptance).

44

Acceptance is not denial or distraction via a whiskey bottle, a family-sized pack of Doritos, or a quick kick of the cat. Acceptance requires you to remain aware of what you are accepting, with an open heart and an open mind. However, as we saw previously, acceptance should not take the place of structural reform. But it might offer us some sort of relief until that structural reform is achieved.

Later in this Survival Guide we will explore different ways you can develop resilience through acceptance.

Wall Four: Self-Care

The final part to the Shelter of Resilience, a solid *Wall of Self-Care*, comprises of the following materials:

- one-part relaxation and physical exercise
- one-part mindfulness
- one-part human connection.

Relaxation and Physical Exercise

What Counts as Relaxation and Physical Exercise?

This is probably the easiest to answer because it is the most common form of self-care.

Relaxation or physical exercise counts as long as you are doing any of the following:

- You are activating your built-in calming system (your parasympathetic nervous system).
- You are deactivating your fight-or-flight state (your sympathetic nervous system).
- You give your body or mind time to recover.
- You stop functioning and you experience the moment once in a while.

- You give yourself a break from your negative thoughts.
- You shift your emotions from negative to positive.
- You give yourself an opportunity to break free from the inactivity that can drag down your emotions and turn your thoughts negative.
- You awaken your mind and body so you feel more alive.
- You give yourself a break from your work or school life, your home life, and any other external pressures.

The Benefits of Relaxation and Physical Exercise. Science says…

Relaxation is not just a nice thing to have; it is essential for your survival, and it will help you to thrive. If your mind and body are repeatedly stressed, without any time to recover, you are more likely to suffer from a wide range of physical ailments such as high blood pressure and heart issues.

When you are stressed, your amygdala fires a signal through the autonomic nervous system (ANS). The ANS contains two different parts: the sympathetic nervous system, and the parasympathetic nervous system.

When your sympathetic nervous system kicks in, this activates the fight-or-flight mode. Fueled by adrenalin
- your heart pumps faster;
- you begin to sweat;
- your pupils dilate;
- your blood pressure increases;
- you are on alert for danger; and
- cortisol is produced (the stress hormone).

If you remain in this stressed state, your brain can actually change, making you more prone to depression and anxiety.

Relaxation exercises or physical exercise can counteract this effect by slowing your heart rate and allowing your brain to function more effectively. You give your body a chance to rest, digest, and heal. For example, studies have shown that yoga and meditation can be beneficial for

- an increase in blood flow to the frontal lobe (the part of the brain that helps us to think more clearly), and
- a decrease in the blood flow to the amygdala (the brain's alarm system).

Mindfulness

What Counts As Mindfulness?

Mindfulness is based on the principles (or attitudes) of
bringing your full attention to the present experience;
nonjudgmental acceptance;
patience; and
trust.

You can use the principles (or attitudes) of mindfulness

- internally, by adopting a mindful approach to your thoughts and emotions;
- externally, by behaving with people and your environment in a mindful way.

But this still sounds a little vague, as if I am asking you to dance in a white nightgown while I play you the sound of a dolphin's cry. So, let's get real, and show you how you can "*do*" mindfulness:

Step 1 – Notice one thing at a time. (Simple, isn't it? No recordings of any sea mammals required.)

47

Step 2 – Really notice your internal and external states, including the colors and textures, and how that makes you feel.

Noticing at this level of detail can give you greater choices about how you choose to respond. When you are mindful, you are less likely to react impulsively.

Noticing in this level of detail, and with this amount of attention, is the opposite of distracting yourself, or trying to "check out" from the present moment, known as *dissociation* (we will explore this further in Chapter 5).

When it comes to noticing what your travel companions are saying, notice the actual words, but also the subtext, the context for what is being said, and the nonverbal communication (for example, facial expressions). Noticing even painful emotions can give you the chance to see that they are only temporary.

In his book *Full Catastrophe Living,* Jon Kabat Zinn describes mindfulness as the practice of "non-doing" and "letting go." When you adopt a mindful approach, your job is to simply become aware of what is going on, without trying to change it, interpret it, or consider how it affects you.

Step 3 – Don't confuse mindfulness with laziness or acquiescence. Some mistakenly claim that mindfulness is like sleepwalking through life, but it actually requires you to remain alert and alive so you can achieve three things:

A State of Full Awareness – Mindfulness requires full awareness of your thoughts, your emotions, and your bodily sensations. This is what distinguishes mindfulness from relaxation exercises:

- Relaxation exercises are an attempt to change our state; we do them to become more relaxed.
- Mindfulness requires us to remain fully aware of our present state without trying to change it; so, we are not trying to become more relaxed.

The State of Full Acceptance – As we saw in the previous section, if we do not fully accept our thoughts, emotions, and bodily sensations, they will make themselves known in the end. Mindfulness requires us to stop ignoring or denying our present state, and fully accept the present reality, no matter how hard that may be.

Informed Change – Once we become fully aware and fully accepting of our thoughts, emotions and bodily sensations, we can stop running on autopilot and start to make informed choices about the changes we need to effect.

Step 4 – Adopt mindfulness even in the most basic of activities, including:

- Having dinner with friends
- Having sex
- Going for a walk
- Tying your shoes
- Filling the dishwasher
- Talking to your travel companions
- Fixing a shelf
- Gardening.

As you have probably guessed by now, you can do pretty much anything mindfully.

The Benefits of Mindfulness.
Science says…

Numerous studies have shown that mindfulness is useful for a wide range of issues including depression and anxiety. Again, research shows that mindfulness helps to
- increase blood flow to the frontal lobe (the part of the brain that helps us to think more clearly); and
- decrease blood flow to the amygdala (the brain's alarm system).

Human Connection

What Counts as Human Connection?

Most would say that human connection is when you feel engaged with someone at an intellectual and emotional level. To connect with someone, you have to show that you value them, though you do not need to agree with their viewpoint to value them. Human connection is a matter of respect for their autonomy. It is not enough to experience that respect at an internal level; the respect needs to be communicated to form a human connection.

Nobody has a continuous, consistent level of connection with someone else. The quality of connection can be influenced by
- how open the other person is to a connection with you;
- what else is going on in your life; it can be hard to remain connected with someone when you are distracted by the prospect of losing your job or dealing with a two-year-old child who is screaming the house down;
- your style of connection to others can also be influenced by how you were raised. For example, if your caregivers were distant, you might think that

50

being distant is a desirable way to be in your adult relationships.

But you can unlearn what your caregivers taught you. In your present life, there might be at least one travel companion who appears open and willing to connect with you in a healthy manner. For more on what makes a healthy relationship, have a look at Chapter 4.

The Benefits of Human Connection.
Science says…

Human connection gives you a reason to live. It soothes you, and it confirms the edges of your personality. You can try and deny it, you can go it alone for a while, but eventually you will need to connect with others.

Studies have also shown that the more we are introduced to new experiences, such as connecting with other people, the more the brain produces dopamine, the feel-good chemical. We can get these new experiences by connecting with brand new people or connecting at a deeper level with people we already know.

The production of dopamine is not guaranteed with every human connection; rather, it depends on the quality of the interaction and your interpretation of the connection. If you interpret the connection as nurturing or empathic, it is likely to produce more dopamine.

Beyond the production of dopamine, neuroscientists have discovered that we learn more, produce more, and are generally happier when we engage in human connection. The new experiences afforded by human connection helps to create new neural pathways in your brain, and can help you to create a new understanding of yourself, others, and the world around you. You can shift your understanding

- from *People are unsafe* to *Some people can offer a certain degree of safety*;
- from *I am unlovable* to *I can be loved by some people*;
- from *I am powerless* to *I have some power over certain things.*

Later in this Survival Guide you will see how you can build your own Wall of Self-Care.

If You Are in Crisis

You are taught never to break glass, but there are times of crisis when you need to do this to activate an alarm. If your Survival Tools are not working, or the walls of your Shelter of Resilience are crumbling, and depression, anxiety, relationship conflict, or trauma is about to make you do something harmful, you are in crisis and you must seek immediate, professional help.

Here are some of the ways you can seek immediate professional help, and I will repeat these in Appendix Crisis, set out at the end of this Survival Guide:

- Call 911 (if it is available in your area).
- Take yourself to the Emergency Room of your nearest hospital.
- Call a friend or family member, and ask them to take you to the Emergency Room.
- Call the National Suicide Helpline on 800-273-8255 / www.suicidepreventionlifeline.org.

Know that when you are in crisis, your brain is less likely to function to its greatest ability. This means that you might only consider a limited list of options when there might be more ways to resolve the problems you are experiencing. This means you should seek help so a trained professional can ensure your safety, and help you get out of your current state of crisis.

Going Beyond the Blue

Let me help you through the wilderness that is life so you can get beyond the blue of the male label. Along the way you may encounter depression, anxiety, relationship conflict, or trauma, and you will have to make difficult decisions. My aim is to offer you as much information as possible so you can make an informed decision at every crossroads you encounter.

So, are you ready to continue your journey beyond the blue?

CHAPTER 2

BEYOND THE BLUE OF YOUR DEPRESSION

There is a beast that dwells in the shadows of all of us. If it were to approach, you would not notice until it landed heavily on your shoulders, until it dragged you down with a solid sense of hopelessness. By the time you feel this weight, it is too late to escape. Your energy, your enthusiasm, and your sense of direction are already being devoured from within.

Enter the Beast

The Beast of Depression is multifaceted and a changeling because it adopts many different forms for different people. For some, the Beast might appear in the form of elongated tears, pining and longing, while others experience short, intense bursts of anger and irritability. Problems arise when people expect the tears but miss the other signs.

Can you recognize the multifaceted Beast of Depression in any of these guises?

- The over-sleeping fatigue of an excessive bed-dweller
- The stooped head of an over-worker
- The dead-eyed smile of the dark-hearted laugher
- The gorging mess of an over-eater
- The dried-up sterility of an under-eater
- The fire and flash of the explosive aggressor
- The wane and drain of the persistently negative thinker
- The deadpan indifference of the flat, numbed-out non-feeler

- The ache, pain and throb to the head, stomach and joints of the somatizer
- The cut and burn of the self-harmer
- The hopelessness of the suicidal
- The disappearing act of the isolator.

In the grip of the Beast, life seems pointless or uninteresting, or you snap at your loved ones, or you know the right things to do to improve your life, yet have zero motivation to attempt any of them. You feel tearful and sad; you cannot remember the last time you easily fell asleep; you have about as much energy as a drained battery; you tell yourself you are a failure, which is proven when you cannot concentrate on a conversation with your partner. You are restless, or you have dark thoughts of hurting yourself; or you buy stupid things hoping they will change how you feel but you cannot be bothered to get that damn Peloton out of the box, let alone read the instruction manual.

The author Margaret Atwood called it "the Sluggish Wave," it was Winston Churchill's "Black Dog," and some have referred to it as a wet rubber blanket. If you have experienced the Beast of Depression, or you have witnessed it in others, I wonder what your pet name would be?

Mental Workout Routine

Use the space below to make a note of the name, and some features, of your particular Beast of Depression. If you have not experienced depression yourself, perhaps you have witnessed it in someone you know. If so, make a note of the name and features of the Beast you have witnessed in that person.

The name of your Beast of Depression (or a Beast you have witnessed in someone else)

```

```

The features of this Beast of Depression (for example, how you recognize it)

```

```

For 3 bonus points – Identify one reason why this Beast is particularly beastly; for example, what makes you want to punch this Beast in the face?

```

```

Subtotal of bonus points so far: _____

The Beast Is Tricky

Unlike other challenges to your mental health, the Beast of Depression is particularly tricky. If you let it take hold, it will trap you in the following double bind:

- You over-estimate the severity or negativity of situations in your life; and
- You under-estimate your own ability to handle those situations.

If you were to compare the Beast of Depression with another challenge to your mental health, for example obsessive-compulsive disorder (OCD), there is no "escape clause" for depression. With OCD, if you follow certain routines (for example, you touch the door handle three times) then your emotional discomfort tends to subside (at least temporarily).

In stark contrast, when you are in the grip of the Beast of Depression, there is no such escape. Every situation proves the double bind that you are either in a severely negative situation, or you are unable to handle it, and so the Beast's grip intensifies.

Mental Workout Routine

Does any of this seem familiar? Make a note of any times when you felt trapped in this double bind, where you felt crushed by the severity or negativity of a situation, and you felt unable to cope.

For 3 bonus points – *Make a note of three specific examples of when you have felt trapped in this double bind of depression. If you have not experienced depression yourself, make a note of what you have witnessed in someone else.*

1.
2.
3.

Subtotal of bonus points so far: _____

The Beast's Trail of Destruction

Why should you be afraid of the big, bad Beast? Less helpful people will try to dismiss your experiences as "a funk" or "just a bad day," but the Beast of Depression leaves a trail of destruction. Here are some of the remnants of this destruction:

- Depression is lethal; research shows that depression is linked to higher rates of suicide.
- Research indicates that depression is linked to cognitive constriction, which means the brain functions less effectively. We are unable to see all options available (hence the link to higher rates of suicide), and so depression means we cannot perform at our full potential at work, in school, or at home.
- The World Health Organization claims that depression is more debilitating than many physical illnesses (for example, tuberculosis and cardiovascular disease).
- Research suggests that caregivers who suffer from depression (without the appropriate help) can have a significant impact on the mental and physical well-being of their children. During the first eighteen years of a child's life, the mental health struggles of a caregiver are considered "adverse childhood experiences," and the higher the number of such experiences for a child, the greater the likelihood of impairments to their mental and physical well-being in adulthood; for example, an increased risk of heart disease, cancer, and strokes.
- With an estimated 264 million people affected by depression worldwide, there is a huge economic cost due to, for example, loss of productivity, healthcare, and other such costs. In the United States alone, some estimate the annual cost of depression to be $210 billion.

- The stigma of depression means that many people who need help do not get the help they need. Unlike many physical illnesses, people who are depressed are sometimes labeled "lazy" or "malingerers."

In short, the Beast of Depression can leave a trail of destruction in your working life, your school life, or your home life. It can severely impact your ability to function at even the most basic level (it seems pointless to eat, for example), and it can threaten relationships with your colleagues, friends, and family.

The Beast is longing to feast on your joy, your confidence, and your self-esteem, so you need to remain vigilant and spot the Beast before it attacks.

Spotting the Beast – Two Vantage Points

Vantage Point 1 – A Bird's Eye View of the Landscape

Don't look just for one feature of the Beast — take a bird's eye view of the landscape. You need to identify a persistent state where the features can be identified. The Beast of Depression does not just give you an off day, when you don't want to get out of bed, or have a flash of explosive anger. An off day is not depression.

The true Beast can be spotted in a persistent state of
- excessive fatigue;
- excessive work;
- excessive laughter or smiles when you feel flattened or numb;
- excessive explosive anger;
- excessive negative thoughts;
- excessive… well, you get the idea.

So, what do we mean by excessive? If any of the above features remain for

- most of the day;
- nearly every day;
- for at least two weeks

more likely than not, you are face to face with the Beast of Depression.

Vantage Point 2 – Don't Confuse the Beast with Your Own Reflection

It is all too easy to look for the Beast and realize you are staring at your own reflection. It is a changeling creature, after all. Don't confuse the Beast with your own tendencies. For example, if you are a naturally introverted person, isolation might be part of your usual routine. For you, a tendency to isolate would not be a sign of the Beast lurking in the shadows.

To truly spot the Beast, you need to identify behavior or patterns that are out of the ordinary. Are you suddenly withdrawing, when you usually feel energized by the presence of others? Are you more irritable or snappy than usual? Are you eating or sleeping more than you usually do?

Help Beyond the Labels

Trying to draw a clear line between "depression" and "no depression" is like drawing a line between one wave and the next. As a result, we need to exercise caution when it comes to depression and diagnostic labels. Depression is a vague state that comes and goes like a fog of dread, so to quantify it, or to expect an accurate definition, is akin to trying to pin a cloud to your lapel. When professionals adhere too rigidly to diagnostic labels, they run the risk of adopting such a narrow interpretation of a person's behavior, thoughts, and emotions that they fail to identify the depression, leaving that person to wander the wilderness alone. As we will see, this risk increases if you are male labeled, and when the male label intersects with aspects of your identity beyond the blue of the male label (for example, due to the racism, transphobia, biphobia, or homophobia of the diagnosing healthcare professional).

Nevertheless, some people find the certainty of labels comforting, and so, for completeness, here are some of the diagnostic labels that are attached to the Beast of Depression.

Major Depressive Disorder

This diagnostic label is sometimes slapped on the Beast of Depression if it lingers for two or more weeks, making you do a number of uncharacteristic things such as persistently overwork, over-eat, under-eat, over-sleep, have outbursts of anger, think negatively, feel hopeless, have suicidal thoughts, feel numb, feel aches and pains, self-harm, or isolate.

Persistent Depressive Disorder, or Dysthymia

If it has been a bad couple of years but you don't quite fit the label of major depression, some professionals might use the label of persistent depressive disorder (dysthymia).

Situational Depression (Adjustment Disorder)

There are times when the Beast will suddenly appear, looking like major depression or dysthymia, but the Beast enters the scene following a certain life event, such as
- unemployment;
- financial difficulties;
- legal troubles;

- a divorce or child custody issues;
- a serious illness;
- a bereavement; or
- other adverse events.

If you experience emotional distress within three months of any of these adverse events, your reaction is out of proportion (for example, you are overwhelmed by the life event, and see no hope of being able to cope), and your emotional distress causes issues at work, at school, or at home, the Beast of Depression would be given the label of situational depression (or adjustment disorder).

Major Depressive Disorder with Seasonal Pattern

There are certain times of year (mainly fall or winter) that can cause the Beast to appear, and this would be labeled major depressive disorder with seasonal pattern.

Major Depressive Disorder with Psychotic Features

Occasionally the Beast will whisper into your ear, making you hear things, or cast shadows, making you see things that are not there. This is psychotic depression, and this is a particularly difficult version of the Beast to manage alone. If you have such experiences, it is important to get the help of a trained professional.

When the Beast attacks, the label is less important than the help you need. Whether or not you fall within any diagnostic label, if you think the Beast is stalking you, trust your instinct and seek professional help. Tips on how to do so follow in this chapter and in Chapter 6.

Formal Assessment Tools

Some professionals use more formal ways to assess depression, and two examples are Beck's Depression Inventory, and the Patient Health Questionnaire 9 (PHQ

9), which, for those who prefer a formal assessment as much as a label, can be found online:

- NCS Pearson Inc. owns the copyright to the Beck's Depression Inventory;
- Pfizer Inc. owns the copyright to the Patient Health Questionnaire 9 (PHQ 9).

The same arguments apply to these tools as apply to labels. Questionnaires, like diagnostic labels, can oversimplify what cannot be simplified. There is a risk that questions will be asked or answered in a way that leaves the Beast of Depression hidden in the shadows. This risk is increased when we consider the Beast and the male label, as well as your identity beyond it.

* * *

Depression and the Male Label

The Beast does not have a preference; it will devour any person of any label. And yet some claim depression is not a threat if you have been given the male label, as if this sex label acts as a magical force field. If this were true, I would be happy to have fewer clients in my psychotherapy practice. But the sad reality is that the Beast of Depression is just as much a threat to the male labeled as to anyone else.

Here are two reasons why:

- According to the National Institute of Mental Health, each year in the United States six million people who are male labeled suffer from depression.
- The rates of suicide are four times higher amongst people who have been given the male label, and suicide and depression are close bedfellows.

The Beast's Large, Dark Underbelly

There is a large, dark underbelly of underreported cases of depression amongst the male labeled. To understand why (at least in part), the American Psychological Association points to a tendency for depression to be thought of in limited ways. If I were to ask how you might describe someone who is depressed, I wonder whether you might describe the following person:

> *Quiet, tearful, reluctant to engage in daily life, or showing no interest in things they would usually be interested in.*

As we saw earlier in this chapter, the Beast of Depression is a changeling that comes in many different guises. Depression can be quiet and tearful, but research shows that it can also arise as explosive anger and irritation, or an incessant need to prove one's self-worth, through, for example, a constant need to overwork.

The Black Swans of the Depressed Male Labeled

If you only expect a white swan, you will never see the black ones, and so when people only expect the depressed to be withdrawn or tearful, that is all they see. The people who are depressed, those around them, and the healthcare professionals who are supposed to help, do not recognize the anger or irritation, the overworking, the incessant need to perform, as symptoms of the Beast of Depression. And so, the large dark underbelly of underreported cases of depression swells and grows fatter, and those in need of help are left to suffer alone.

The Societal Myth of the Depressed Male Labeled

The majority of this dark underbelly of underreported cases is due, in part, to a societal myth that the male labeled do not suffer from depression. This is simply not true, and yet I have encountered therapists, psychiatrists, and doctors who continue to perpetuate this myth. They focus on the surface behavior of their male labeled clients, and instead of trying to understand the depression fueling that behavior, they refer dismissively to their male labeled clients as "narcissists," "sociopaths," or "examples of toxic masculinity." I have even heard these professionals say, without any sort of scientific justification, that the male labeled are inherently unable to experience emotions in the same way as the female labeled, and some professionals claim that the male labeled are inherently violent and aggressive.

As we saw earlier in this Survival Guide, there is a higher rate of diagnosis of the male labeled when it comes to externalizing disorders such as oppositional defiant disorder, conduct disorder, and other such diagnoses. Some argue such diagnoses are given to the male labeled at a higher rate because the male label blinds the diagnosing healthcare professionals to other potential diagnoses, such as depression. It is also arguable that, due to the racism, transphobia, biphobia, or homophobia of the diagnosing healthcare professional, this issue is compounded when we consider a person's identity beyond the blue of their male label.

The Conditioning Associated with the Male Label

We also don't notice the black swans of the depressed male labeled because of the way we are conditioned. All of us, no matter our label, are taught certain things about the male label. Some examples of what we are taught (explicitly or implicitly) include:

- We expect the male labeled to be silent and strong, and thus not admit to vulnerabilities. Depression is the king of vulnerabilities, and so shame silences you.

65

- The male labeled are expected to focus outwards, on external gain and power, not inwards, on emotions and thoughts. As a result, you may be unaware that what you suffer is depression.
- The male labeled are expected to remain independent, and so seeking help for something like depression is an admission of defeat. As a result, fewer male labeled are likely to access mental healthcare for depression, and so the myth continues that the male labeled are somehow untouched by the Beast.
- Due to structural inequality, the problem of a lack of access to mental healthcare by the male labeled is compounded when we consider how the male label intersects with a person's identity (for example, racial or ethnic identity, true gender identity, or sexuality).

As the United States is a patriarchal society, this conditioning influences the dominant view of emotions. The approach preferred by many with power or authority is to focus outwards, on achievement and power. Depression, anxiety, and trauma are all rather inconvenient truths that many people would rather not hear about.

As a result of conditioning, we don't expect the male labeled to have emotions or vulnerabilities, and if we do witness it, it conflicts with our expectations. We don't want to hear about it. Cognitive dissonance requires that we ignore this inconsistency or turn it into something else. As a result, we expect to see more anger and aggression from the male labeled, and less emotional distress and fewer cries for help.

Sometimes I wonder whether this conditioning is a form of heroic fantasy. Perhaps we are taught these myths about the male labeled to offer us an illusion of security; surely the Beast is not that lethal if our strong male labeled heroes can remain impenetrable to it. And for the few male labeled who do succumb to depression, we can perhaps blame them for failing to stay strong and stoic. It is easier to blame the individual than to accept the reality of a Beast of Depression waiting to overpower people of any sex label.

The trouble with fantasies is that at some point, we must wake up and accept reality. And while we were fantasizing and daydreaming, the Beast might have edged a little closer.

The Way We Respond to the Black Swan of the Depressed Male Labeled

As we saw above, healthcare professionals interpret people's behavior, and that interpretation is vulnerable to bias. But it isn't just healthcare professionals who do this.

In a study carried out by researchers John and Sandra Condry (1976), research participants watched the same video of a baby crying. Half the participants were told the baby was labeled male and interpreted the baby's crying as anger and frustration. The other half of the participants were told the same baby was labeled female, and they interpreted its crying as distress and fear.

Thus, the label impacted the participants' interpretation of the infant's behavior. And our response to a person's anger and frustration is usually more defensive and less supportive than our response to someone we perceive as scared and in distress.

Mental Workout Routine

Are you aware of this sort of conditioning attached to the male label? Or have you witnessed it in others?

Consider also whether this conditioning has arisen regarding the intersection of the male label and your identity (for example, your racial or ethnic identity, true gender identity, or sexuality). For example, have you experienced structural inequality when attempting to access mental healthcare? Have you experienced any racism, transphobia, biphobia, or homophobia of a healthcare professional?

Do you think any of this has had an impact on your depression (or the depression you have witnessed in others)?

In the space below, make a note of three examples where you have witnessed this.

1.

2.

3.

Survival Tools to Tackle the Beast

So far in our journey together, you have learned how to spot the Beast of Depression, you have seen the trail of destruction it leaves, and you have been reminded of how the male label can blind us to the Beast, even when it is standing right in front of us.

Time to reach for those handy Survival Tools introduced in Chapter 1. But there is one snag; the Beast of Depression is nimble enough to use your Survival Tools against you, and if you are not quick-footed in response, it will ensnare you in a beastly cycle of depression.

- <u>Your Action Pack</u> — As the shadow of the Beast descends, it makes you retreat, and so you do less of the things that once made you feel good.

- <u>Your Head Gear</u> — The less you do, the fewer positive experiences you have to brighten your thoughts, and so you become more negative in your thinking. Trapped in inactivity, your Head Gear may start to develop faults; for example, you believe your lack of engagement with life is proof that you are a "hopeless cause."

- <u>Your Flashlight</u> — For fear of the Beast, you dim the Flashlight to a dull glow, as dull and dark as the thoughts that were starting to circle. You believe you are hopeless, so you feel hopeless, you do even less, and see yourself in a less positive light.

And so, the beastly depression cycle continues.

Figure 8 - The Beastly Depression Cycle

But the Beast does not have to win. The more familiar you are with your own Survival Tools, the easier it will be to master them to break free of the cycle of depression.

* * *

Survival Tool #1 – Action Pack (Behavior)

Old, New, and Borrowed, to Get you Beyond the Blue

Remember from Chapter 1 that the first of your Survival Tools is your Action Pack. You can engage in actions and behaviors that once made you feel good (the "old"), or you can create new experiences from your own brainstorming (the "new"), or from ideas that are borrowed from others (the "borrowed").

Also remember the importance of including new ideas in your Action Pack: more new experiences mean more dopamine, the feel-good chemical, and more new experiences means the creation of new neural pathways. If you want to keep yourself safe from the Beast of Depression, new actions might help create a new understanding of yourself and the world around you; you might acquire evidence that you are capable and resilient, and the world is not so overwhelming.

Mental Workout Routine

Use the space set out below to answer the following questions. These are designed to help you identity the components to your own Action Pack. Ideally you should have at least five actions to help you feel better – we are aiming for at least one for each weekday.

- *What has made your heart race with excitement in the past? What is likely to again? What ideas do you have from other people to create this state?*

- *What has created a glow of contentment in the past? What is likely to again? What ideas do you have from other people to create this state?*

- *What has filled your eyes with stars of joy in the past? What is likely to again? What ideas do you have from other people to create this state?*

- *What sparked your mind with interest in the past? What is likely to again? What ideas do you have from other people to create this state?*

[ ]

- *What has opened doors of hope in your mind in the past? What is likely to again? What ideas do you have from other people to create this state?*

[ ]

- *What has left your feet solidly placed on the ground, with a sense of presence? What is likely to again? What ideas do you have from other people to create this state?*

[ ]

- *Is there any other behavior that you have engaged in that once made you feel good? If so, list it here. What is likely to again? What ideas do you have from other people to create this state?*

[ ]

Lighten the Load of Your Action Pack

Remember that we don't want to overload your backpack; an incomplete to-do list will simply trap you further in the double bind of depression where you over-estimate life's challenges, and under-estimate your own ability to handle them.

You can lighten the weight of your Action Pack by disposing of any components that do not pass at least one of the following tests introduced in Chapter 1:

1. *The Test of Mastery* — Will the components to your Action Pack develop a sense of mastery?

2. *The Test of Opposite Attraction* — For example, if your Beast of Depression takes the form of the stooped head of an over-worker, a component to your Action Pack would not pass this test if it involved extra work assignments that are borne out late into the night.
Instead, you could try something that would create a slower, calmer sense of presence, for example, a meditation, or a mindful walk around the block.
And if your Beast of Depression takes the form of the over-sleeping fatigue of an excessive bed-dweller, a component to your Action Pack would pass this test if it involved something that is high energy and brings up your heart rate, such as power walking or another form of light exercise.

Remember that an attempt to evoke emotions opposite to those evoked by the Beast of Depression is one approach to breaking the depression cycle. Another way is to mindfully accept, without judgment, the emotions you are currently experiencing. We will explore this further when we look at the Flashlight Survival Tool.

3. *The Test of Appreciation* — Do the components to your Action Pack make you appreciate all that you have?

Create a short list of the components to your Action Pack that pass either the Test of Mastery, the Test of Opposite Attraction, or the Test of Appreciation

A SMART Action Pack

So you think you are all Action Packed and ready to tackle the Beast of Depression? Not so fast. It is all very well making a list of potential actions, but are you being SMART about it?

Mental Workout Routine

If you need to remind yourself how to create a SMART Action Pack, have a quick look at Chapter 1.

Choose at least three components to your Action Pack and use the blank grid set out below (Figure 9) to assess whether each component is SMART.

If it is not SMART, what could you add to make it a SMART Action?

Don't forget to also use the blank schedule below (Figure 10) to make each component to your Action Pack Time-bound.

Item from your Action Pack	Specific ?	Measur-able?	Achiev-able?	Realistic ?	Time-bound? Use the Action Planner below to create a schedule for each SMART Action item

Figure 9 - How to Make Your Action Pack SMART

To make each component to your Action Pack Time-bound –

Component to your Action Pack	Time	Day, and frequency	Intensity
Example - Going for a walk with your partner	Example - 1pm, when the kids are at their activities	Example - Saturdays only, once every two weeks	Example - 20 minutes minimum, 1 hour maximum

Figure 10 - How to make your Action Pack Time-bound

As we saw in Chapter 1, of the three Survival Tools you carry, the Action Pack is the quickest and easiest way to break the Beastly Depression Cycle. The trouble with the Action Pack, however, is

- it doesn't always work against the nimble Beast;
- it may only work for a short time;
- it may not get to the root of the depression; and
- it may mask important information your emotions are trying to communicate to you.

This is why we also need the other Survival Tools to help break the depression cycle.

* * *

Survival Tool #2 – Head Gear (Your Thoughts)

Your Head Gear – your thoughts, beliefs, and assumptions about yourself, others, and the world around you – can help or hinder you when it comes to the Beast of Depression. It really depends on what you do with this essential Survival Tool.

Figure 11 - The Beastly Depression Cycle

So, let's first familiarize ourselves with our Head Gear and the common faults that can arise.

As Simple as A-B-C

Remember the ABC log from Chapter 1? Here is another copy, to refresh your memory (Figure 12).

As we examine each component of the ABC log, we will explore the case of Charles, someone who is male labeled, and has been struggling with depression for years.

As you learn about Charles, you will get a chance to fill out your own ABC log for your own depression, or for depression you have witnessed in someone else.

A	B	C	D	E
Activating Event	Beliefs & Assump-tions	Conse-quence	Dispute	Evaluate

Figure 12 - ABC Log

Column A – The Activating Event (or Trigger)

You will recall that the activating event refers to what was happening at the time of your depression, or at the time you noticed its presence.

When you noticed the Beast was weighing heavily on you

- Were you with a travel companion who tends to criticize you?
- Was there yet another dispute at work, where criticisms were thrown around the board room?
- Did you notice that you were not going to the gym as much recently, or eating too much garbage?
- Have you been overscheduling your time with work or activities for the kids, and failing to allow for any time for rest or relaxation?

Don't worry if you cannot identify specific activating events. If your depression just lingers, causing a vague sense of negativity or irritability, use column A to record noteworthy times when you felt particularly negative or irritable.

Remember, the focus is just on what is happening. Save any beliefs or assumptions for column B of your ABC log.

Example
Charles didn't really notice the Beast arrive, but all of a sudden, they felt its heavy weight. Charles's version of the Beast often made them irritable with their family, and Charles tried to cope with the guilt and hopelessness by eating too much late into the night.

Although Charles didn't think this was the sole trigger, Charles wrote in column A of their ABC log the activating event of losing out on a promotion at work. This had been a long and drawn-out process, and all for nothing.

Ever since, Charles had been finding it hard to sleep, which made little things seem even worse. Just that evening, the dishwasher stopped working, and Charles smashed a glass into the sink in a rage, giving up on the evening entirely, and retreating to bed at eight o'clock.

Mental Workout Routine

Think of the last time you were depressed. Even if there was not one trigger, identify the activating event by answering these questions:

- *What was going on? (For example, were you at work or home, and what were you doing there?)*
- *Who was involved?*
- *Was there anything out of the ordinary about what you were doing, or what others were doing around you?*

If you have not experienced depression yourself, answer the above questions if you have witnessed depression in someone else.

Now have a go at filling out column A of a blank ABC log (use the log at Figure 12).

Column B – Your Beliefs and Assumptions

As you saw in Chapter 1, we need to use the ABC log to identify any beliefs or assumptions that you had at the time of the activating event. This will help us to identify if your Head Gear (the way you are thinking) has developed any faults.

Example
Remember Charles? They were snapping at their family, eating too much late into the night, having trouble sleeping, and they smashed a glass into the

sink when the dishwasher stopped working, all at the same time as they were denied a promotion.

When they were denied a promotion at work, Charles *assumed* this was because Charles was incompetent. This is like feeding a Beast of Depression a pre-workout and a four-course dinner.

When the dishwasher broke, Charles *assumed* the dishwasher was beyond repair, and they used this and the lack of promotion to support their *belief* that they are a "failure."

Mental Workout Routine

Now have a go at filling out column B of the ABC log, identifying any beliefs and assumptions you made about your own activating event. If you witnessed the depression in someone else, try to work out what sort of beliefs and assumptions they were making.

For any belief you identify, rate the strength of your belief on a scale of 1 to 7, where
      1 = you don't really believe it, and
      7 = you wholeheartedly believe it.

This rating will serve as a baseline when we dispute and re-evaluate those beliefs in columns D and E of the ABC log. If you are filling this out for someone else's depression, try and rate on a scale of 1 to 7 how strongly they seemed to hold those beliefs.

Remember that numerical ratings can help give things a focus, and research indicates that when people see an improvement (even if that is only reflected numerically), this can help inspire further improvement in mood.

Two Levels of Faulty Head Gear

Your beliefs and assumptions can make you more or less vulnerable to the Beast of Depression, depending on how faulty your Head Gear is.

We can develop faults at two different levels:

Level 1 – The Contextual Level (for example, your interactions, and the role of others) -

> When Charles found out that they had missed out on their promotion, they started to think about how they came across at work. Charles assumed their colleagues thought that Charles was a jackass, and so Charles assumed this was the reason Charles had missed out on the promotion. Charles went on to assume their position was now untenable, and Charles should leave the company.

Charles's Head Gear has developed faults at this first, contextual level because:

- Charles assumes they did not get the promotion because of their relationship with their colleagues. However, a whole range of other factors is involved with awarding a promotion, and some of those factors have nothing to do with Charles (for example, the business could be going in a different direction, or there are political factors involved in the decision-making).
- Charles's assumptions might be based on misinformation. For example, Charles might have misinterpreted certain facial expressions of certain colleagues when, in reality, those facial expressions might have had nothing to do with Charles. Just as we question whether a newborn baby's smile is joy or just trapped wind, a range of

reasons could explain the facial expressions of Charles's colleagues.

- Charles's assumptions might be over-stating the case. For example, a handful of Charles's colleagues might find it irritating when Charles does certain things, but they wouldn't label the whole of Charles's personality as *jackassery*.
- Charles's assumptions might be unfairly generalized. For example, perhaps only one or two colleagues think that Charles is a jackass, not the whole company.

Level 2 – The Core Level (Self-image).

Whether or not Charles's colleagues think Charles is a jackass, how does this impact Charles's view of their core quality? Does Charles believe they are, to the core, "a jackass" or "a failure," or "a bad person"?

Often when we look at this level of fault in our Head Gear, we realize these core beliefs cut across other contexts in our life. So, Charles might also view themself as a jackass, failure, or bad person when it comes to their parenting, their intimate relationship with their partner, or their place in their wider family tree.

Seven Common Faults in Your Head Gear

No matter which of the two levels, the faults tend to be the same. Psychiatrist David Burns refers to these as "twisted thinking," which I particularly like, but others have called them "cognitive distortions," "maladaptive thinking," and "unhelpful thought patterns."

No matter the name, the seven most common faults that undermine your Head Gear are:

1. All-or-Nothing Thinking

All-or-nothing thinking is like cutting off your nose to spite your face; you will not accept a middle ground, and so you adopt assumptions and beliefs such as

- *I can never make a mistake;*
- *If we do not share everything with each other, we have no relationship;*
- *If I do not get perfect grades, school is a waste of my time;*
- *If I do not get that job, I am not going to succeed in anything I do.*

In this faulty, black-and-white thinking, there is no shade of grey, no room for doubt, and no hope of compromise. Many people think this way, but it is particularly common if you have experienced trauma. In such a case, it is likely that you experienced a loss of control, which was probably extremely distressing. So why would you be willing to compromise? Only when you see that this sort of thinking does not make you any more safe, and rarely leaves you in any state of greater control of your life, are you willing to let go of this rigid approach.

Does any of this sound familiar to you?

Mental Workout Routine

Using the space set out below, make a note of times when your Head Gear suffered from the fault of all-or-nothing thinking.

Pay particular attention to any times when you felt that this fault worsened your depression.

If you cannot think of a time when you experienced this, make a note of when you witnessed it in someone else.

```

```

2. Emotional Reasoning

When you allow your emotions to influence your thoughts, you engage in *emotional reasoning*. Some examples include:

- You feel stupid, so you think that you are.
- You feel sad, so you believe you are more wounded than you really are.
- You feel guilty, so you end up living in a way that makes you, or other people, believe you did something wrong.
- You feel hopeless, so you see few options available.

Faults like this develop when the oil, grease, sweat and blood of your experiences start to clog, rust, or rot the usually smooth functioning of your Head Gear. You feel so much that you cannot think straight, and so you start to believe that what you feel is the whole picture.

Mental Workout Routine

So how about you? Did you feel stupid, so you believed it? Did you feel lonely, so you believed you had no one in the world? Using the space below, note the times when your Head Gear suffered from the fault of emotional reasoning.

If you cannot think of a time when you experienced this, make a note of when you witnessed it in someone else.

```
┌─────────────────────────────────────────┐
│                                         │
│                                         │
│                                         │
│                                         │
└─────────────────────────────────────────┘
```

For 3 bonus points - Make a note of one example of when this fault made the depression worse (your own or the depression you witnessed in someone else).

```
┌─────────────────────────────────────────┐
│                                         │
│                                         │
│                                         │
└─────────────────────────────────────────┘
```

Subtotal of bonus points so far: _____

3. Putting the "Ass" in Assumptions

In this fault, instead of finding out all the facts, we fill the gaps of missing information with *assumptions*, which are usually negative. For example:

- You stop talking to a friend because you assume they did not invite you to a party because they don't like you. (Turns out, their partner invited all of their friends, and there was no room for your friend to invite anyone.)
- You assume the person who never says hello to you is rude and thinks you are stupid (when, in reality, they are intimidated by you because they think you are really smart).
- You assume that your partner wasn't listening, and so you feel like you are not worthy of anyone listening to you, when in reality, they were trying to order you a birthday gift.

Part of making assumptions includes mind reading; this is when you fill in the gaps by assuming you know someone else's motives or intentions.

You know what they say about making assumptions? It makes an ASS out of U and ME. So check whether you have all the information.

Mental Workout Routine

Using the space set out below, make a note of times when your Head Gear suffered from the fault of putting the ass in assumptions. Pay particular attention to any times when you felt that this fault worsened your depression.

If you cannot think of a time when you experienced this, make a note of when you witnessed it in someone else.

4. The Tyranny of the Shoulds

Psychoanalyst Dr. Karen Horney coined the phrase "the tyranny of the shoulds," and psychotherapist Dr. Albert Ellis used the less appealing "musturbation." No matter what you call it, many people find that their Head Gear misfires when they place too much emphasis on how things *should* or *must* be in life. For example:

- *I should perform perfectly at work, or at school.*
- *My friends must not leave me out of their plans for the weekend.*
- *My boss should speak to me in a less hasty manner.*
- *Life should be fair.*

The greater the number of shoulds and musts, and the harder we hold onto them, the more shocking the fall will be when life fails to meet all our expectations.

And when we fall from such a great height of expectation, we are more vulnerable to the Beast of Depression.

Mental Workout Routine

Using the space set out below, make a note of times when your Head Gear suffered from the fault of the tyranny of the shoulds. Pay particular attention to any times when you felt that this fault worsened your depression.

If you cannot think of a time when you experienced this, make a note of when you witnessed it in someone else.

For 3 bonus points - Make a note of one example of when this fault made the depression worse (whether it was your own depression, or that of someone else).

Subtotal of bonus points so far: _____

5. Personalization

Me, me, me, it is all about me! No, not narcissism. In fact, the opposite; you believe you are at fault, or inadequate, or failing at every moment. This is the fault in your Head Gear that is called *personalization*.

Here are some examples:

- You don't get that promotion, and so you believe it is because of your incompetence.
- There is a dispute in your family, and you think that you are solely to blame.
- There is a pandemic, and you believe only you are going to get this mysterious airborne virus.
- Your children are not doing well at school, and so you stay up all night, searching for ways you could have done things differently.

Personalization is about an overemphasis of your role in the situation that is creating your distress. You do not see that there may be other people, or other factors, that might have led to the current state of affairs.

Mental Workout Routine

Using the space set out below, make a note of times when your Head Gear suffered from the fault of personalization. Pay particular attention to any times when you felt that this fault made your depression worse.

If you cannot think of a time when you experienced this, make a note of when you witnessed it in someone else.

6. Catastrophic Thinking

Remember the double bind of depression? You
- overestimate a potential threat; and
- underestimate your ability to handle it.

Well, *catastrophic thinking* is a type of fault in your Head Gear that is all about the first part of this double bind.

Some examples of catastrophic thinking:

- When you see a crack in the wall, you don't just think about filling it, you *believe* the whole house is going to fall down.
- When your boss frowns at you, you don't believe they are struggling to find just the right words to compliment you. Instead, you assume this frown means you are going to get sacked.
- When your child comes home with a grazed head, you just know they are going to have swelling on the brain later that night.

Mental Workout Routine

Using the space set out below, make a note of times when your Head Gear suffered from the fault of catastrophic thinking. Pay particular attention to any times when you felt that this fault made your depression worse.

If you cannot think of a time when you experienced this, make a note of when you witnessed it in someone else.

For 3 bonus points – *Make a note of one example of when this fault made the depression worse (whether it is your own depression, or whether it was witnessed in someone else).*

[blank box]

Subtotal of bonus points so far: _____

7. Dodgy Filter, Overgeneralizations, and Labeling

You filter out the good, and you focus on the bad. As a result, you overgeneralize one bad experience to multiple times in your life, incorrectly assess your life as all-bad because you have filtered out the good moments, and label yourself a "failure" or "loser", thus leaving yourself even more vulnerable to the Beast of Depression.

Here are some examples of the fault of a dodgy filter, overgeneralizations, and labeling:

- You miss the train and you label your entire life a "disaster".
- You cannot sleep because of the money you lost on one bad business deal.
- You decide you can never again trust a friend because they made one mistake.

Mental Workout Routine

Using the space set out below, make a note of times when your Head Gear suffered from the fault of a dodgy filter, overgeneralizations, and labeling. Pay particular attention to any times when you felt that this fault made your depression worse.

If you cannot think of a time when you experienced this, make a note of when you witnessed it in someone else.

Example
Remember Charles? What faults can you identify in Charles's Head Gear? Using the space below, list three faults that you can identify, and the reasons for this. (The answers follow.)

1. Name of fault in Charles's Head Gear:

Reasons:

2. Name of fault in Charles's Head Gear:

Reasons:

3. Name of fault in Charles's Head Gear:

Reasons:

```

```

Answers

- *Charles **personalized** the situation with the promotion, and the dishwasher. As we will see in the next section (when we discuss column D of the ABC log), numerous reasons can explain these unfortunate incidents. It is not all down to Charles and their competence.*

- *Charles demonstrated **catastrophic thinking** by assuming the dishwasher was beyond repair, and by generalizing this one event to a conclusion that Charles's whole life has fallen apart.*

- *Charles's Head Gear was also suffering from the fault of a **dodgy filter** because they focused on their lack of promotion and the dishwasher breaking to distort their perspective to an overly negative view of their life. They filtered out anything positive, **overgeneralizing** these two setbacks, and **labeling** themself a "failure."*

  Incidentally, Charles rated their belief "I am a failure" as a 6 out of 7, which is pretty high. We will use this as a baseline later on when we try to fix the faults in Charles's Head Gear. We will do this in column D of the ABC log when we dispute Charles's faulty beliefs and assumptions, and then in column E, when we re-evaluate how much Charles still believes that they are a "failure."

First, however, we need to turn to the next column of the ABC log.

Column C — Consequences (Emotional and Behavioral)

As a result of the activating event that you noted in column A of the ABC log, and the beliefs and assumptions you noted in column B:

- **How do you feel?** (the *emotional consequences*)
  If you feel depressed, how would you rate that depression on a scale of 0 to 10, where
  - ○ 0 = not depressed at all, and
  - ○ 10 = intensely depressed.
  In the case of Charles, they rated their depression to be a fairly high 7 out of 10.

- **What did you do (or not do)?** (the *behavioral consequences*)
  In the case of Charles, you saw how they smashed a glass in the sink and went to bed early. Perhaps this meant they did not have a workout that night, or they didn't get time to hang out with their partner, and each of these might have made them feel worse.

Mental Workout Routine

Turn again to the blank ABC log (Figure 12).

Previously, you filled out Column A (the activating event) for when you were last depressed (or for when someone you know was last depressed).

You also filled out Column B for the beliefs and assumptions that you (or someone else) held about that activating event.

Now have a go at filling out column C of the ABC log, making a note of the emotional and behavioral consequences of that activating event.

For the emotions – remember to include a rating of the intensity of that emotion, on a scale of 0 to 10, where
- *0 = not depressed at all, and*
- *10 = intensely depressed.*

This will serve as a baseline to compare with how you feel after you have disputed and re-evaluated the beliefs and assumptions you initially made. More of that when we get onto column E.

For now, we need to try and fix the faults in our Head Gear.

Column D – Disputing or Correcting Faulty Beliefs and Assumptions

To use your Head Gear to break the depression cycle, you need to fix any faults in your Head Gear.

As you saw above, there are seven common faults that undermine your Head Gear, and so we will look at how we can fix each of them.

1. All-or-Nothing Thinking

To fix this particular fault, you need to learn to think in terms of shades of grey. Does it have to be all or nothing, or is there a middle ground that you could tolerate?

Here are some additional things to consider:

- To take an absolutist standpoint, you better be pretty damn sure of your facts. The trouble is, in life we rarely have all the facts all of the time. So, it seems safer to adopt a more flexible approach: allow for the possibility that we could be wrong, that we may not have all the facts, and that there may be an alternative perspective.

For example, if someone makes a mistake, that one mistake does not mean that person can never be trusted again. You might watch this person a little more closely, but do they need to be thrown to the dogs? After all, if you throw everyone to the dogs, you will end up isolated, and the Beast of Depression loves to pick off the isolated stragglers. Find safety in numbers, forgive, and drop such absolute, perfectionistic standards.

- To adopt an all-or-nothing or black-and-white perspective often gives us the security of certainty. The trouble is, life is too unpredictable to reduce it to the binary opposites of black or white. At some point, we will have to come to terms with our discomfort around uncertainty.

2. Emotional Reasoning

To fix the fault of emotional reasoning, you need to realize that your emotions are an important source of information, but they do not rule the show. In particular:

- Emotions should be balanced with other sources of information, including logic, proportionality, and an analysis of all the facts.

- Just because you feel like a failure, isolated, or hopeless does not mean that any of this is true.

- The enormity of an emotion can overshadow other factors, so always take the time to ask yourself:

What else am I missing by listening too much to this particular emotion?

- Parent Yourself: Your emotions might be ruling the moment because of your wounded "inner child." For example, if you were sent away to boarding school at eleven years old, and you interpreted this as a lack of love from your parents, you might still hold that sense of feeling unlovable.

No matter how much you try some adult rationalization, your inner eleven-year-old will still cry out, "But I feel unlovable, so therefore I am!" In Chapter 5, we will explore various ways to overcome feeling stuck in the past, but in the meantime, try these two steps to fix the fault of emotional reasoning:

Step 1 - Connect with your inner child. Really communicate respect to that inner child, and accept that what they felt back then was valid. As a child, it was scary to feel unlovable, especially if you felt unlovable in the eyes of your parents, upon whom you had to rely for such basic needs as food and shelter.

Step 2 - Only when you have connected with your inner child and validated their feelings can you then gently show that inner child all the ways their emotions are not applicable to life in the present, as an adult. For example, you might be able to point to a loving and supportive partner who is the polar opposite of the parents who once sent you away to boarding school.

- As mentioned earlier in this Survival Guide, neuroplasticity is a wonderful thing, so by parenting yourself, you are teaching your old dog brain new tricks. By connecting with your inner child and validating their emotions, you are creating new neural pathways, and your emotions do not need to be so big to be heard.

3. Putting the "Ass" in Assumptions

Want to have great Head Gear that works well in any given storm? Stop making an ass of yourself with all those assumptions. In particular:

- Check whether you have all the information necessary to form a particular conclusion. Do you really know you were left out of the meeting because your fellow directors are planning to terminate your position at the company? Or are there legitimate reasons why your presence was not needed?

- Ever seen the David Cronenberg movie *Scanners* in which people could read each other's minds? Do you know or remember what happened? People's heads started to explode. It was a horror movie for a reason; we really don't want mind readers in this world, so stop trying to pretend you have that canny ability to scan another person's mind. You do not know, for sure, someone's thoughts or motives. You can find out by asking them, but until you hear it from the horse's mouth, stop making assumptions about what is in someone else's mind.

4. The Tyranny of the Shoulds

To truly fix your faulty Head Gear, you need to eradicate "should" and "must" from your vocabulary. In reality, your "should" or "must" is likely to be a preference rather than an essential prerequisite for your survival. In particular:

- You would "like" someone to turn up on time, as I am sure you would "like" to be able to do the same for that person. But even if your hopes and expectations do not come to fruition, you will probably survive. You may even thrive on the experience by learning something new as a result of things not turning out how you think they should.

- The more cognitive flexibility you can develop, the healthier you will be. Think about how nimble Luke Skywalker was when he jumped over the Great Pit of Carkoon (*Return of the Jedi*); in the same way, if you drop the shoulds and musts, you will free yourself of impossibly rigid standards that just cannot match up to the reality of life's perpetual uncertainty. We cannot possibly predict what will occur — whether it's the cat pooping on the carpet, or the children throwing a hissy fit in the supermarket — but if you roll with it, you will soon be flicking your light saber in defeat of the Beast of Depression. Better than falling into the Great Pit of Carkoon.

Mental Workout Routine

*Identify a must or should in your life. For example, you might say to yourself, I **must** present at that work conference, or I **should** invite those neighbors over for a drink, or I **must** call my parents.*

Use the space set out below to make a note of your particular must or should statement.

98

Now make a note of what you could be doing instead of what you noted above. Call this the Replacement Fun Task. For example, you could be taking your kids on a hike instead of doing that thing you believe you really must or should do.

Make a plan to do the Replacement Fun Task. By what time/day are you going to do it?

5. Personalization

To fix the fault of personalization, you can evaluate your own role in everything that happens in your life, but only if:

- You also consider the other factors that influenced the outcome. This list depends on the context, but here are some of the factors that could have been involved:

    - the involvement of other people
    - the needs of a company (if, for example, it is an issue in the workplace)
    - economic forces (such as the state of the job market)
    - nepotism
    - structural challenges, such as racism, transphobia, biphobia, or homophobia
    - the possibility that you do not have all the facts involved in influencing the result

- You accord your own involvement weight equal to any other factors that influenced the outcome.

6. Catastrophic Thinking

To fix the fault of catastrophic thinking, you need to accept that there will be few catastrophes in your lifetime. As a result, you need to:

- Turn down the volume on your reactions to the spilled wine, broken door handle, unexpected bills, missed exit for the shore, and the neighbor who accidentally ran over your newly planted row of trees.

- Save your catastrophic language for the true catastrophes, such as the terminal illness or death of a loved one.

- In between, other events have varying degrees of consequences, and so our language, and our reactions, should be scaled down to proportionately reflect the degree of severity of those consequences.

- Even for the true (and rare) catastrophes, it is a mistake to allow the fault of all-or-nothing/black-and-white thinking to discolor reality. Such catastrophes may involve difficult and painful experiences, but may also offer small gems of hope, wisdom, or even peace.

7. Dodgy Filter, Overgeneralizations, and Labeling

Remember the Black Swan analogy; if we only look for, and thus only see White Swans, that does not mean no Black Swans exist. The same can be said for the positive experiences in your life; they are there, just waiting to be remembered as they politely clear their throat backstage. They are just longing to be called into the limelight for their swan song.

To help fix your dodgy filter, search for those positive experiences by doing these five things:

1. When you finish a task, do not review it without making note of at least one thing that you did well.

2. Make a list of your positive experiences, taking note of the qualities about you that made that experience so positive.

3. Get a friend or loved one to help you add to that list.

4. Stick the list where you can see it, and remind yourself daily of the good, to balance against the not-so-good.

5. Challenge the absolute rigidity of labels. For example, what do you mean by a "failure" or "loser"? So you made one mistake. What about all the things you have done well? Don't they negate those labels?

Example

Mental Workout Routine

You will recall how Charles struggled with the faults that undermined their Head Gear.

Using the space set out below, make a note of how you can fix Charles's faulty Head Gear.
(The answers follow.)

1. Tips to fix the fault of Charles's personalization

2. Tips to fix the fault of Charles's catastrophic thinking

3. Tips to fix the fault of Charles's dodgy filter

Answers

1. To fix the fault of personalization, Charles could depersonalize the lack of promotion by recognizing that reasons other than Charles's competence were at play. For example, the business might have been undergoing restructuring or financial difficulties, or internal politics could have been in play.
With regard to the dishwasher, the manufacturer might have produced a defective product, which had nothing to do with Charles.

2. To fix the fault of catastrophic thinking, Charles could check the information they have and resist jumping to an extreme conclusion. For example, perhaps Charles wasn't promoted because their manager has them in mind for an even better promotion, one that better reflects their experience and skill set.
And perhaps the dishwasher is not broken beyond repair, but only needs a slight adjustment.

3. To fix the dodgy filter fault, instead of generalizing one or two seemingly negative experiences to the whole of their life, Charles could take a more balanced view and review some of the good and bad things that make up their life. This might help to lead Charles away from the belief that their whole life is falling apart.

Mental Workout Routine

Turn again to the blank ABC log (Figure 12) and now have a go at filling out column D. Try to fix any faulty Head Gear you identified in column B of the log. Were there any examples of
- *all-or-nothing/black-and-white thinking;*
- *emotional reasoning;*
- *putting the ass in assumptions;*
- *the tyranny of the shoulds;*
- *personalization;*
- *catastrophic thinking;*
- *dodgy filter, overgeneralizations, and labeling?*

Column E - Evaluating Beliefs and Emotions

Now that you have fixed the faults in your Head Gear, you can re-evaluate your beliefs and emotions.

Re-evaluate your beliefs
Remember that in column B of the ABC log, you identified beliefs and assumptions, and you rated each belief on a scale of 1 to 7?

How would you rate those original beliefs now, on a scale of 1 to 7, where
> 1 = you don't really believe it, and
> 7 = you wholeheartedly believe it

You will recall that Charles initially held the belief that they were a "failure," and they rated this as a 6 out of 7.

After they fixed the faults of their Head Gear, they re-evaluated this belief to be a lower 2 out of 7.

In column E, you might also create a new, more constructive belief to replace the above-mentioned belief. Try to give this new belief a rating from 1 to 7, where
      1 = you don't really believe it, and
      7 = you wholeheartedly believe it.

For example, instead of Charles holding vehemently onto the belief that they are a "failure," they were willing to entertain the more constructive belief that "I am a hard worker." Charles rated this as a 4 out of 7.

Re-evaluate your emotions
Remember that in column C you recorded the original score, on a scale of 0 to 10, for your depression (or the depression of the person you know).

Now you have used column D to fix the faults in your Head Gear, how would you rate your depression on a scale of 0 to 10, where
      0 = not depressed at all, and
      10 = intensely depressed?

If you are doing this for someone else, how would you imagine their depression level has changed as a result of fixing the faults in their Head Gear?

The theory is that you may, eventually, see a decrease in this level of distress.

Example

After Charles challenged their beliefs and assumptions in column D, they rated their depression to be a much lower 2 out of 10 (when it had initially been a 7 out of 10, when recorded in column C).

You can find a completed example of the ABC log for Charles in Figure 13.

Mental Workout Routine

Turn again to the blank ABC log (Figure 12). Previously, you filled out columns A, B, C, and D for when you were last depressed (or for someone you know).
Now have a go at filling column E by:

1. Re-evaluating any original beliefs and assumptions (that you identified in column B) on a scale where
    1 = you don't really believe it, and
    7 = you wholeheartedly believe it

Create a new, more constructive belief to replace the above-mentioned (unhelpful) belief. Try to give this new belief a rating from 1 to 7, where
    1 = you don't really believe it, and
    7 = you wholeheartedly believe it.

2. Re-evaluate your depression (that you identified in column C) on a scale of 0 to 10, where
    0 = not depressed at all, and
    10 = intensely depressed
If you are doing this for someone else, how would you imagine their depression level has changed as a result of fixing the faults in their Head Gear?

The theory is that you may, eventually, see a decrease in this level of distress.
Continue to monitor yourself and reflect on how you are progressing with this.

A	B	C	D	E
Activating Event	**Beliefs & Assumptions**	**Conse-quences**	**Dispute**	**Evaluate**
Example – Losing out on a promotion at work	*Example –* Charles personalized the situation with the promotion, and the dishwasher.	*Example -* Emotional consequence – Charles feels a 7 out of 10 level of depression.	*Example -* Deperson-alize the promotion: There are many other reasons for this.	*Example -* Old belief ("I am a failure"): Believe it at a 2 out of 7
	Charles also demon-strated catastrophic thinking by assuming the dishwasher was beyond repair, and by general-izing this event to an assumption that Charles's life is falling apart.	Behavioral consequence s – Charles smashed a glass in the sink and went to bed early.	To fix catastrophic thinking: Am I missing any information? To fix the dodgy filter, instead of generalizing one or two negative experiences, carry out a balanced review of the good and bad.	New belief ("I am a hard worker"): Believe it 4 out of 7. Depression: 2 out of 10
	Charles used a dodgy filter by filtering out anything positive and labeling themself a "Failure." Charles' belief "I am a Failure" = 6 out of 7			

Figure 13 - Completed ABC Log

Eight-Point Check of Your Head Gear

Caught out in the wilderness of life's journey, and with the Beast of Depression prowling, you need to be quick on your feet. So here is a quick eight-point check of your beliefs and assumptions, so you can use your Head Gear to break free of the depression cycle as quickly and easily as possible -

1. Identify the Type of Faults in Your Head Gear
Whether it is all-or-nothing thinking, a scarlet heart of emotional reasoning, or the blushed cheeks of personalization, you have to identify the fault before you can fix it.

2. Prove It or Lose It
Weigh up the evidence for and against that particular fault, and make an informed judgment.

3. Flex your Flexibility
A rigid approach is likely to snap crucial components in your Head Gear. Soften a little so you can develop cognitive flexibility in two ways.

a. Flex your Flexibility by challenging any fixed role that has been allocated to you. We all do it, because life is too busy to really get to know the minute detail of every single person we interact with. So we shortcut the process by allocating roles:
- You are over-stretched and neglecting your home life because at work or school you are seen as the "can do" person (who ends up with everyone else's work).
- You are frustrated into a voiceless and opinionless silence because you are viewed as the "quiet one" (even when you have a boat load of things to say).

107

- You want to collapse with exhaustion because you are seen as the "energetic one" (who ends up coaching everyone's kids even when struggling with an ankle injury).

Whatever the role that has been allocated to you, flex your flexibility by stepping out of that role every now and again:
- You can say no to coaching every now and again.
- You can say yes to a work presentation, even if the loud member of your team is set to explode with all the things they want to say. Even the most introverted person can have a day of interest in other people.

b. Flex your flexibility by challenging your assumptions. We have already seen how assumptions make an ASS out of U and ME, so resist making assumptions about
- yourself;
- others; and
- the world around you

4. Watch Your Language
Is it really a catastrophe? *Should* you, or would you *prefer* to? *Must* you, or would it be *nice* to? What do you mean by a "failure"? And how have you been a "success"? These labels are too simplistic to tell the full story, and we human beings are far more interesting than that.

This is not just about semantics even if you, as do I, enjoy a bit of word play. The reality is that the way you label things makes a big difference when it comes to how you feel, and what you do (or don't do) in response.

5. Scale It Down
Context is all, so devise a scale of distress from 0 to 100. Initially, you may have felt that losing out on that business

deal was the end of the world, and you will surely be crushed by the Beast of Depression. But, after a good night's sleep, you can see that, compared with the 100 out of 100 of one of your children dying, losing out on that deal is a mere 20 out of 100.

6. Phone A Friend
Ask people you trust whether they would think in this way in the same circumstances.

7. Talk to Yourself
Replace that negative, critical voice with the sort of kind, fair voice you would use with your children, loved ones, or friends.

8. Cost-Benefit Analysis
Weigh up the cost versus the benefit of leaving that particular fault in your Head Gear unfixed.

* * *

As you scale back your language, as you notice more of the positives, as you stop labeling yourself, and you stop scaring the daylights out of yourself with your catastrophic thinking, you may notice the quiet retreat of the Beast of Depression. It will see that you are not beating yourself up over the smallest of errors, and so you deftly slip free of the double bind of depression by
- not over-estimating the severity or negativity of situations in your life; and
- not under-estimating your own ability to handle those situations.

Your Head Gear, if used correctly and with the faults fixed, can be a most useful Survival Tool to break the depression cycle. But what If the Beast of Depression continues to prowl, trapping you with that dull ache of gloom? Fear not, for you still have one more Survival Tool to try.

* * *

Survival Tool #3 — Flashlight (Your Emotions)

Remember that in Chapter 1 you were introduced to a Flashlight that is your emotions. You can learn how to use this valuable tool to light your way out of the Beastly Depression Cycle.

Component 1
The Multicolored Words of the Flashlight

When the Beast of Depression stalks you, you need to be familiar with your Flashlight's first component:
The full spectrum of the multicolored emotion words.

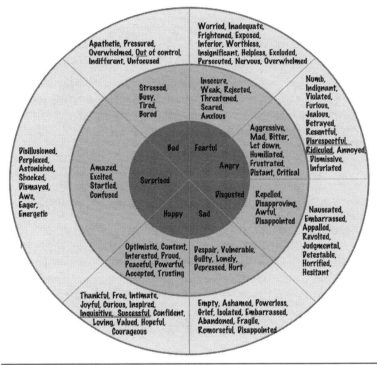

Figure 14 - The Full Spectrum of Your Emotions

Example
Dwayne had been brought up in a household where emotions were expressed using a fist to Dwayne's face.

As a result, Dwayne spent years punching holes in walls because they had few emotion words to communicate their distress. This dead-end experience left Dwayne stuck, without any idea how to progress, because all they ever felt was an aching pain of apparent anger inside their chest. The more violent Dwayne's outbursts became, the more negative their thoughts became, and this only darkened the Flashlight of Dwayne's already dimly glowing emotions. Dwayne was trapped in the cycle of depression.

When Dwayne turned 18, they moved out of their abusive childhood home, and found freedom at university. There they met people who were aware of the wide spectrum of emotions, and Dwayne finally learned that the aching pain inside their chest was not anger but the emotions of loneliness and fear.

With the help of new friends, Dwayne learned to communicate loneliness and fear, and in response, the friends offered support and kindness. An expression of loneliness and fear is more likely to evoke a softer response than an expression of anger.

Deeper friendships were forged because Dwayne no longer scared people away with angry outbursts, and Dwayne learned to calmly and assertively communicate a wider spectrum of their emotions.

To become familiar with their Flashlight, Dwayne had to appreciate that it was multicolored; there was a whole spectrum of emotion words (as shown in Figure 14) beyond the binary of "angry" or "indifferent."

But to name the emotion is only the half of it. Dwayne also needed to identify the intensity of that emotion. For example, Dwayne learned to rate the intensity of their emotion on a scale of 0 to 10, where –
0 = A very low, flatlined level of intensity, and

10 = An intense, mushroom-cloud level of intensity

As you will recall from Chapter 1, the intensity of your emotions depends on a number of different sources of power, so let's review what powers this important Survival Tool.

Component 2 - The Power Pack in Your Flashlight

Your Flashlight needs fuel to power it, and so the intensity of your emotions will depend upon the amount of power you can get from a number of different sources, including sleep, food, drink, drugs, exercise, and the absence of stressful experiences.

Mental Workout Routine

To use your Flashlight wisely, ensuring you will survive and thrive in the wilderness of your life, you need to understand when your own power pack might become depleted. We all have our own rhythms; some need more or less sleep, some are more or less sensitive to alcohol, and some need more or less exercise.

Knowledge is power, so use the grid set out below (Figure 15) to identify your own patterns in the intensity of your depression. If you have not experienced depression yourself, think of someone who has, and use the grid to identify their patterns.
The patterns of intensity will be identified by keeping a note of
- *sleep schedules;*
- *what is consumed (food, drink, drugs);*
- *any exercise;*
- *the accumulation of stressful experiences over a recent period;*

- *the extent to which you have over/under-scheduled yourself.*

Day	Sleep Schedule	Consumption of food, drink, and drugs	Exercise	Stressful experiences?	Over/ Under scheduled?
Monday					
Tuesday					
Wednesday					
Thursday					
Friday					
Saturday					
Sunday					

Figure 15 - How to Master the Intensity of Your Flashlight

Component 3 — Master the Dimmer Switch

As mentioned in Chapter 1, there are times when you need to adjust the intensity of your emotions, so you need to learn how to master the Dimmer Switch on the Flashlight. To master it and regulate your emotions, use any of the following techniques:

grounding exercises,
breathing exercises
visualization exercises.

Mental Workout Routine

*Stimulate Your Five Senses (**A Grounding Exercise**)*

In brief, a grounding exercise is a means to keep you firmly in the present, without getting distracted by past regrets or the dread of the future. You may, for example, feel disconnected, and so you need to do things to turn that Dimmer Switch up a little, and feel more connected to your surroundings and the people in your life.

If the Beast of Depression has squeezed all enjoyment out of you, leaving you feeling disconnected or depleted, you can turn up the Dimmer Switch on your emotions by engaging all five senses.

Take a moment, stop what you are doing, and follow the five steps set out below. Once you have completed this exercise, use the space provided to make a note of what you noticed in your emotions, thoughts, and bodily sensations.

1. Notice and describe to yourself five things you can see. Notice the colors, textures, shapes, and shadows.
2. Notice and describe to yourself four things that you can touch. Run your hands over them, noticing the smoothness, roughness, bumpiness, and the heat or coolness of each item.
3. Notice and describe to yourself three things that you can hear. Notice the loudness or softness of each sound, and allow the sound to reverberate in your ears. How does it feel to hear each sound?
4. Notice and describe to yourself two things that you can smell. What is it like to smell each of these? What does each smell evoke in you?

5. Notice and describe to yourself one thing you can taste. Savor the taste, and just let it rest in your mouth for a little. What is that like?

```
┌─────────────────────────────────────────┐
│                                           │
│                                           │
│                                           │
│                                           │
└─────────────────────────────────────────┘
```

For 3 bonus points - Award yourself 3 bonus points if you manage to engage in this exercise at least once a week within the next three weeks.
Subtotal of bonus points so far: _____

*Engage Your Breathing Apparatus (**A Breathing Exercise**)*

You might wonder why you have to pay any attention to your breathing apparatus. After all, you have been carrying around your set of lungs for the whole of your life. But this breathing apparatus offers you an amazing way to adjust the Dimmer Switch on your Flashlight.

Psychiatrist Stephen Porges proposed the "Polyvagal Theory," which emphasizes the importance of breathing exercises to activate the ventral vagal nerve network, your built-in social engagement system that triggers calmness. It is essential that you find more and more opportunities to stimulate this nervous system because it reduces the harmful production of cortisol, the stress hormone. We will look more at Polyvagal Theory in Chapter 5.

As we saw with the five senses exercise, engaging your breathing apparatus can also ground you in the present moment, turning your attention away from the negativity and self-criticism that are the hallmarks of the Beast of Depression. When you focus on each breath, you turn down the Dimmer Switch on the intensity of your despair, ceasing to overestimate potential threats and underestimate your own ability.

Take a moment to just stop what you are doing, and follow the following steps. Once you have completed this exercise, use the space set out below to make a note of what you noticed in your emotions, thoughts, or bodily sensations.

1. Notice each breath as it comes in through your nostrils, and out through your lips. Notice what the temperature is like as the breath comes in through your nostrils. Is it cooler compared with the breath as it goes out through your lips?
2. Notice what the slight pause is like between the inward breath and the outward breath.
3. Try to breathe into your diaphragm rather than your chest. You can make sure you are doing this by placing a hand gently over the space at the top of your belly, just beneath your rib cage.
4. If your mind wanders, refocus on your breath by imagining a ribbon (of your chosen color) going in through your nostrils, down into your body, and then out through your lips.
5. Try to double the length of your outward breath compared with your inward breath (for example, two seconds inwards, four seconds for the outward breath).
Alternatively, try square breathing: Two seconds inward, hold for two seconds, outward breath for two seconds, hold for two seconds, and then continue to repeat this process of perfect symmetry.

For 3 bonus points - *Award yourself 3 bonus points if you manage to engage in this exercise at least once a week within the next three weeks.*
Subtotal of bonus points so far: _____

Activate The Power of Your Imagination (*A Visualization Exercise*)

Adjust the Dimmer Switch on the Flashlight by using the power of your imagination. In short, visualize images that will help you to regain control over what might be an intense emotion.

Take a moment to stop what you are doing, and follow the following five steps. Once you have completed this visualization exercise, use the space set out below to make a note of what you noticed in your emotions, thoughts, or bodily sensations.

1. Visualize the Beast of Depression trying to prevent you from achieving your goal. For example, you are desperate to get fit, and yet the Beast blocks you at your front door, mocking you by prodding your softening belly. "They will all laugh at you," it snarls with a curl of the lip.

2. Now visualize yourself shoving that Beast aside and walking out of the house, getting quickly to your car so you can drive straight to the gym without a second to ponder your options. Notice your surroundings in this visualization: Is the sun shining? Do you enjoy the smell of fresh air as you picture yourself leaving the house?

3. Continue this visualization all the way to the gym, and imagine what that feels like to work up a sweat, and grind those heavy weights.

4. Even better, notice how you feel when you visualize the end of a whole hour at the gym as you walk out, feeling more energized and enthusiastic.

5. You may notice feelings or thoughts of resistance to the goal (perhaps you have a twist of fear in your stomach, or the Beast is still whispering, "You are bound to fail"). If this is the case, try to focus on your breathing to lessen the fear, and repel the Beast's comments by refocusing on every aspect of this visualization: the colors and textures of the images, the sounds, the smells, and so on. The more realistic the visualization feels, the easier it is to imagine fulfilling that future goal. And so the heavy weight of helplessness is lightened by this technique to adjust the Flashlight's Dimmer Switch.

For 3 bonus points - Award yourself 3 bonus points if you manage to engage in this exercise at least once a week within the next three weeks.

Subtotal of bonus points so far: _____

Surf the Light Waves of each Emotion

As mentioned in Chapter 1, you do not always need to adjust the Dimmer Switch on your Flashlight. Sometimes you need to keep it at its current setting, and use it to light your way. Even if the emotion that is evoked by your Depression seems a little unsettling, remember the temporary nature of emotions; there is a buildup, a peak, and then it subsides (see Figure 16 for a reminder of this).

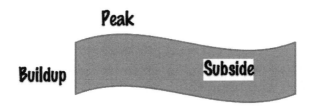

Figure 16 - How to Surf the Light Waves of Your Emotions

By staying with the emotion, you teach your brain that this emotion is not some blinding light that will burn you to the core, and by staying with it, you can survive and thrive, despite the sadness or loneliness.

* * *

So Far in Our Journey Together

So far we have identified the Beast of Depression, considered how the Beast is a threat to the male labeled, and explored how to use your three Survival Tools to break the cycle of depression.

Life's journey through the wilderness is long. It is exhausting to constantly use these Survival Tools to break yourself free of every depression cycle. There comes a point when you need to rest, and the safest way to do this is inside a Shelter of Resilience.

* * *

Your Shelter of Resilience

You will recall from Chapter 1 that we need four walls to build the Shelter of Resilience:

- Self-Compassion
- Self-Esteem
- Self-Awareness through Acceptance
- Self-Care.

Wall One: Self-Compassion

The Beast of Depression tricks you into believing that you are defective, and that you have no hope of making anything better. It hardens your inner voice so you end up talking to yourself as if you are your own worst enemy:

One or two mistakes are overgeneralized so that everything you do is wrong.

You quickly forget the times of strength and achievement.

You only see the moments of weakness and failure.

To soften this inner voice, let's try a quick exercise.

Mental Workout Routine

You will recall that compassion consists of kindness, a wish to see an end to suffering, knowledge that we are all human and capable of making mistakes, an understanding approach rather than judgment, and a mindful, balanced approach to life.

For each of these hallmarks of compassion, think of a time when you adopted this compassionate attitude towards one of your travel companions (for example, your partner, friend, family member, or colleague). Using the space set out below, make a note of the words you used to express this compassion (whether it was spoken or simply thought about).

Kindness

```



```

A wish to see an end to suffering

```



```

An acceptance of someone's mistakes

```



```

An understanding approach, rather than critical or punitive

```



```

A mindful, balanced approach

```



```

Now you have tuned your brain into a more compassionate voice, try to create that compassion for yourself.

Use similar words you used above to comment on an incident where you were self-critical.

Use the space set out below to record compassionate words about that incident.

You can choose a different incident for each component to compassion, or use the same example for each.

Self-kindness

A wish to see an end to suffering for myself

An acceptance of my own mistakes

An understanding approach, rather than self-critical or self-punitive

A mindful, balanced approach to my actions

Ten-point Check of Your Wall of Self-Compassion

Mental Workout Routine

By now you might be convinced that this Wall of Self-Compassion is essential for you to survive and thrive. But will it stand up against the Beast of Depression?

Carry out this ten-point check to test the strength of your Wall of Self-Compassion.
For each statement, rate how true it is for you, where

0 is it is never true,
all the way up to 4 points, where you believe that
statement is always true for you.

	Never 0 points	Rarely 1 point	Half of the time. 2 points	Most of the time. 3 points	Always 4 points
1. When things go wrong, I tend to blame myself					
2. I find it hard to accept that I have done something well					
3. I criticize myself					
4. I rarely compliment myself					
5. I don't deserve rewards or things to make myself feel good					
6. I think over and over about things					

Beyond the Blue

	Never 0 points	Rarely 1 point	Half of the time. 2 points	Most of the time. 3 points	Always 4 points
that might have gone wrong					
7. I use absolute language such as "I can never make a mistake" or "I should know this."					
8. I label myself a "Loser" or "Idiot"					
9. When I think of my self-talk, I talk in a way that I would not talk to my children, partner, or any other loved on					
10. I believe that self-criticism					

125

	Never 0 points	Rarely 1 point	Half of the time. 2 points	Most of the time. 3 points	Always 4 points
keeps me on track with my goals.					
Add up your total: The lower the score, the stronger your Wall of Self-Compassion					

Figure 17 - Ten-point Check of Your Wall of Self-compassion

Beast-Proofing Your Wall of Self-Compassion

Even if your Wall of Self-Compassion is pretty weak, you can use these five methods of reinforcement. You will recognize some of these techniques from the faults we identified in our Head Gear. As with the Head Gear, we need to continuously maintain this Wall of Self-Compassion, checking for cracks and faults that might develop over the course of time.

1. Neither right nor wrong, but somewhere in between

When you review your daily performance at work or school, or how well the weekend went with your partner and friends, do you focus on the things you could have done differently? Most of us do this because we are trained to focus on what we did wrong. But we can learn as much from the things we did right. It is all a matter of balance.

Next time you evaluate how well you have been sticking to that diet, or your gym routine, or getting on with coaching those pesky Little Leaguers, you are not allowed to finish that review without picking out one good thing about your performance.

2. Learn from those mistakes

Bill Gates, Richard Branson, Oscar Wilde, and many more wise and successful people have proclaimed the virtue of making mistakes. We try, make mistakes, learn, and finesse the process.

We forgive our youngsters for wobbling on their bike for the first time, or walking around with shoes on the wrong feet (despite telling them twenty times which way around they should go), because we know that they are learning. Why can we not afford ourselves the same grace? Granted, we are not wobbling on our bike, or wearing shoes on the wrong feet, but even if we are investing in the wrong stock, making the wrong judgment call at work, and forgetting our partner's birthday, those mistakes may hold valuable lessons.

3. Watch your language

Notice when you catastrophize: Do you tend to label things a "complete disaster" or "urgent"? Are you the kind of person who impatiently drums your fingers while someone finishes producing the document you need "ASAP"? If so, take a breath, slow down, and really think about whether this is urgent, and whether it will be a catastrophe if things don't work out the way you envisioned.

Also, pay special attention to the language you use; for example, notice when you use harsh, judgmental phrases such as "I am a failure" or "I completely messed that up."

4. As flexible as a yoga instructor

A lack of compassion, self or otherwise, often comes from a lack of flexibility. We have rules about how life *should* be, referred to, as we saw earlier, as the "tyranny of the shoulds" or "musturbation.*"

You want life to go a certain way — which may say more about your fears and insecurities than your need to be a megalomaniac — but the more flexible you can be, the better chance you have of maintaining a Beast-proofed Wall of Self-Compassion.

5. Emails of Self-Compassion

Mental Workout Routine

*Use the space set out below to draft an email to yourself (**Email #1**). This email needs to cover the following —*

Focus on one aspect of yourself that you dislike. This could be your manner when you talk to people, your facial configuration, or the way you approach your job. Whatever it is, don't hold back and go into full asshole mode when you describe your perceived inadequacy.

When you write about your perceived inadequacy, consider the following things:
- *What images come to mind when you think of it?*
- *What do you feel?*
- *What does it make you think of?*
- *Does it remind you of anything or anyone?*

*After you have drafted Email #1, draft a reply (**Email #2**). Pretend this reply is written by someone who really cares about you, who loves you and wants the best for you. If no* *such person exists, imagine that person does really exist. This email needs to cover the following —*

- *Try to express (from the point of view of this friend or loved one) love for and acceptance of you. What qualities does that person see in you, what do they really love about you, or find funny, interesting, comforting? Go into full loving mode.*
- *Really think about the language they would use, and the*
  - *images;*
  - *the feelings;*
  - *the thoughts; and*
  - *any stories about you.*

Leave the exercise for a break, no more than half an hour, and then just read the email of compassion (Email #2).

For 3 bonus points - Award yourself 3 bonus points if you manage to draft Email #1 and #2 within the next week.

Subtotal of bonus points so far: _____

Email #1

To:
From:
Subject:

Dear:

Email #2

To:
From:
Subject:

Dear

Wall Two: Self-Esteem

Mental Workout Routine

How do you rate your self-esteem? We are not talking about how you feel at a given moment; that would be too context driven.

How would you rate yourself when you look at the whole of you, for the whole of your life, putting aside spikes of unusual circumstances?

Record your thoughts using the space set out below.

```
┌─────────────────────────────────────────────┐
│                                             │
│                                             │
│                                             │
│                                             │
└─────────────────────────────────────────────┘
```

Signs of Low Self-Esteem

Can you remember some of the signs of low self-esteem listed in Chapter 1? If not, have a quick look at those to remind yourself.

Mental Workout Routine

Do any of these signs of low self-esteem (as listed in Chapter 1) sound familiar to you? Record your thoughts using the space set out below.

```
┌─────────────────────────────────────────────┐
│                                             │
│                                             │
│                                             │
│                                             │
└─────────────────────────────────────────────┘
```

For 3 bonus points — *Award yourself 3 bonus points if you make a note of 3 specific examples for your thoughts.*

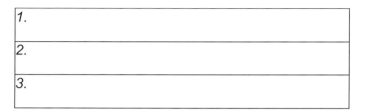

Subtotal of bonus points so far: _____

Strengthen the Wall of Self-Esteem

To strengthen your Wall of Self-Esteem, you have to learn how to cope with life's ups and downs. This means that you need to make use of all three Survival Tools that you encountered in Chapters 1 and 2 (your Action Pack, Head Gear, and Flashlight).

<u>Qualities and Achievements</u>

You also need to acknowledge your qualities and achievements. I get it, the last thing you want to do is become a self-congratulatory jackass who starts every sentence with "I" or "My." So you talk down your qualities and achievements, and you do this so much that your self-esteem is not just on the floor, it is plummeting straight down to the earth's core.

So appreciate the difference between
    Healthy modesty, and
    An unhealthy erosion of your self-esteem, leaving you
    prone to the Beast of Depression.

Mental Workout Routine

Healthy modesty does not mean that you deny the existence of your qualities and achievements. Rather, make a list of these, post it in your home, and then celebrate your qualities and achievements.

Your brain holds onto what you choose, and because we are taught not to turn into a self-congratulatory jackass, we discard our qualities and achievements, and choose instead to hold onto
- *the time we missed the mark by spilling someone's drink; or*
- *the time we said something that slightly upset someone; or*
- *the other time when we fell over drunk at a cousin's wedding.*

If you were raised by a jackass, you are even less likely to hold onto your qualities and achievements. The jackass who raised you taught you to focus on how wonderful they claim to be, and so your own qualities and achievements may seem irrelevant to you. But they are far from irrelevant. In fact, they are essential for you to survive and thrive in the wilderness of your life.

So use the chart below to:
- *Make a list of your qualities and achievements*
- *Highlight the particularly difficult achievements*
- *Choose a way to celebrate those particularly difficult achievements*
- *Print the list and stick it up somewhere in your home so you can continue to strengthen your Wall of Self-Esteem.*

Qualities	Achievements	Difficult achievements	Method of Celebration

Figure 18 - How to Strengthen Your Wall of Self-Esteem

Wall Three: Self-Awareness through Acceptance

As we saw in Chapter 1, you can build the Wall of Self-Awareness by developing an awareness of your Survival Tools, but you also need to develop an acceptance of the things you cannot change.

Mental Workout Routine

There are numerous exercises for developing acceptance, and many of them are based on mindfulness. We will look at mindfulness more when we construct the fourth and final Wall of Self-Care.

For now, try this simple exercise (Parts 1 and 2, set out below) to help you develop self-awareness through acceptance.

Part 1 — Self-Awareness
Have a look back through this Survival Guide and review the answers you have given so far for each Mental Workout Routine. Can you identify any common themes or patterns about the way you use your Survival Tools?

Your Action Pack — What are the common themes or patterns that you have identified in your behavior? For example:

Do you tend to pack your schedule with numerous activities, or

> *are you more a quality over quantity kind of person?*

Do you tend to engage in activities that involve lots of people, a few, or

> *do you prefer just you, you, and only you?*

Do you prefer high-energy activities, or

> *are you more sedentary?*

Using the space below, make a note of at least three examples of any common themes or patterns in your behavior.

1.

2.

3.

Your Head Gear — What are the common themes or patterns that you have identified in your thought process, beliefs and assumptions? For example:

Are your thoughts generally self-critical, or

Negative, or

> *Overly rigid?*

Do you catastrophize, or

> *Label, or*
> *Filter out the good?*

Using the space below, make a note of at least three examples of any common themes or patterns in your thought process.

1.

2.

3.

Your Flashlight - *What are the common themes or patterns that you have identified in your emotions? For example:*
Do you tend to feel sad, or
Lonely, or
Angry, or
Misunderstood?

Using the space below, make a note of at least three examples of any common themes or patterns in your emotions.

1.

2.

3.

Part 2 — Acceptance
As you reviewed the list above, you might have recalled situations where you could not change a problem, no matter how much you focused on your behavior, thought process, or emotions.

Please choose an example of such an unchangeable problem. For example, it might be a problem that
leaves you feeling stuck;
causes you emotional distress;
prevents you from progressing in your career; or
acts as an obstacle in your personal relationships.

Using the space below, make a note of your unchangeable problem.

Focusing on the unchangeable problem that you noted above, follow these seven steps to self-awareness through acceptance:

Step 1 — Carve out a moment when you will not be disturbed. Put your phone on silent, and turn off any distractions (for example, music and television). Don't worry, this won't take long, and the world will keep turning even if you don't check your phone for a few minutes. Keep the unchangeable problem out of your mind for the time being (you can imagine placing it in a box in another room of your home).

Step 2 — Settle into a comfortable position, either sitting or lying down. Rest your attention on your breathing, noticing each breath as it comes in through your nose, and out through your mouth; just allow for the natural rhythm. Focusing on your breathing anchors you in the present moment. For now, there is no point ruminating on the past or fearing an unknown future. Simply focus on the present, with the aid of each breath as it comes in through your nose, and out through your mouth. Any time your mind starts to wander, gently bring it back to each breath.

Step 3 — **Your Body**. Turn your attention to your body. From top to toe, scan each part of your body with attentiveness, but do not let yourself get hijacked by any part of your body. You might notice pain, tightness, or other strange sensations, but do not give those parts of your body any more attention than the rest. Simply notice, and then move on through your body.

Step 4 — **Your Thoughts**. Now turn your attention to your thoughts. Notice any distracting thoughts about the work that is piling up, or the argument you had with your partner last night, or the kids you need to collect from school. Just notice those but do not hold onto them or follow them. Simply notice thoughts as they arise, and let them float away like bubbles. If you have trouble letting the thoughts go, bring your attention back to your breathing and the present moment.

Step 5 — **Your Emotions**. You can now shift your attention to your emotions. You might feel angry, sad or bored by the exercise. Whatever you feel, just notice it, without giving it any particular emphasis, and without making any sort of interpretation, and then gently bring your attention back to your breathing.

Step 6 — **Your Unchangeable Problem**. Now you can turn to the one thing you cannot change, the unchangeable problem you noted above. If you placed it in an imagined box, imagine taking it out of the box and just look at it. Notice it, but do not give it too much attention. Then imagine it is another one of those *thought bubbles, and let it float away as you bring your attention back to your breathing.*

Step 7 — Continue to refocus on each breath as your mind is hijacked temporarily by bodily sensations, distracting thoughts, emotions, or an unchangeable problem. The more you can bring your attention back to each breath, the more you have taught your brain to accept the unchangeable.

Wall Four: Self-Care

To truly keep the Beast of Depression out, you need to erect and maintain one final wall of your Shelter of Resilience. You will recall from Chapter 1 that your Wall of Self-Care should consist of the following:

- One-part relaxation and physical exercise
- One-part mindfulness
- One-part human connection.

Build Your Own Wall of Self-Care

Mental Workout Routine

The Beast of Depression might be just around the corner, so you need to build your own Wall of Self-Care.

Use the blank planner below to decide when you are going to engage in some self-care. You know that a solid wall comprises one part relaxation and physical exercise, one part mindfulness, and one-part human connection, but beyond that, the detail is up to you. I have included a number of mindfulness exercises at www.chriswarrendickins.com , and you can receive more by following the link to sign up - http://eepurl.com/gD41jr

Try not to set yourself up for failure by setting your expectations too high. Start slowly, perhaps a handful of minutes each time a few times a week and build the wall from there.

Day	Relaxation and Physical Exercise	Mindfulness	Human Connection
Monday			
Tuesday			
Wednesday			
Thursday			
Friday			
Saturday			
Sunday			

Figure 19:How to Build Your Wall of Self-Care

* * *

Beyond the Beast of Depression

Before we leave the Beast, we need to acknowledge three secrets about the Beast of Depression.

Secret One: For Some, the Beast of Depression Holds an Allure

Not everyone runs in fear of the Beast. For some, it holds an allure that is hard to resist. There are three reasons why this might be so:
1.   *The Beast is familiar* — If it is all you have ever known, you fear that if you are not depressed, what else are you?

2.   *The Beast is a protector* — You might believe that if you don't have the Beast, you might fall victim to a worse fate. Who dares to hope for the light and warmth of joy when they fear being burned by such an overwhelming emotion? Better to stay in the dank and dark shadow of the Beast.

3.   *The Beast was something you were given and expected to keep* — To maintain a balanced family system, you might have been allocated the role of the "depressed one," the "problem child," or the "scapegoat." To step out of this role might be quite frightening, and there might be others in your life who try to prevent you from getting better.

All of this is an illusion. The Beast might be familiar but it is not essential for your existence. And the Beast certainly isn't there to protect you. If you reveal yourself very slowly to the light and warmth of joy, you might discover that you can survive the Beast, and you might even thrive in this new experience. You do not have to accept the role you were given as a child; experiment a little with a new way, to find what is right for you.

Secret Two: Just When the Beast Seems All-consuming, It Can Disappear

I have worked with male labeled people who have been caught by the Beast of Depression and, no matter how hard they fought, they could not defeat it. Then, all of a sudden, the Beast disappeared, and seemingly for no reason.

No one can really say what motivates the Beast to appear or disappear. If they claim to know the answer, they are selling you snake oil. All you can do is make sure your three Survival Tools are in order, and you keep your Shelter of Resilience as fortified as possible.

141

Secret Three: The Beast Never Dies

We might keep the Beast at bay, but it will never die. The sad reality is depression often returns. But the more adept you are with your Survival Tools, and the stronger your Shelter of Resilience, the quicker and easier you will recover.

* * *

If You Are in Crisis

If you find yourself beyond the blue and the Beast of Depression is about to make you do something harmful, you are in crisis and you need to seek immediate, professional help. Turn to Appendix Crisis for further information.

* * *

Survive and Thrive Recap

In this chapter you

- learned how to identify the changeling that is the Beast of Depression;
- witnessed the trail of destruction left by the Beast;
- identified two vantage points to spot the Beast before it attacks;
- explored the myths surrounding depression and the male label, including the intersection of the male label with your racial or ethnic identity, true gender identity, or sexuality;
- learned how to use three Survival Tools to break free of the depression cycle:
  - o your Action Pack (behavior)
  - o your Head Gear (thought process, beliefs and assumptions)

- o your Flashlight (emotions);
- learned how to construct and maintain the four walls of your Shelter of Resilience:
  - o Self-Compassion
  - o Self-Esteem
  - o Self-Awareness through Acceptance
  - o Self-Care.

We need to let our imagination go beyond the blue of the male label. If we can imagine that human nature is more complex and more unique than ascribed labels, we will open our minds to the fact that the male labeled can and do suffer from depression.

Recognizing this, we can identify the warning signs being communicated to us. And then more people will get the help they need, and we will have a safer, healthier society for all, before it is too late, before we are lost beyond the blue of depression.

CHAPTER 3

BEYOND THE BLUE OF YOUR ANXIETY

As you make your way through the wilderness that is your life, you might encounter a *Fireball of Anxiety* that swirls in shades of

- unanswered emails from your boss;
- thoughts of speaking to people at a social gathering;
- having to ask the mechanic to check your car again, as you are sure there is an undetected fault; or
- unaddressed issues with your intimate partner.

As you feel the heat of this Fireball, your chest becomes heavy, your skin pricks with sweat, your face flushes, and your hands shake.

Behold, the Fireball of Anxiety

It is okay to live with a little bit of worry, but too much can whirl a Fireball into your heart and mind, leaving you unable to focus on anything. Here are some of the reasons why you might identify anxiety in your own experiences:

- You get stuck on a loop as you ruminate over the smallest things.
- You fear a catastrophic experience in the near future.
- You underestimate your ability to handle a situation.
- You assume others are better than you.
- You believe you must perform perfectly.
- You see a dark future where there is the same suffering.

- You assume you will always fail.
- You assume others will always treat you badly.
- You have trouble sleeping.
- Your shoulders and neck are stiff.
- You often have an upset stomach.
- You have bowel issues such as diarrhea or constipation.
- You notice that you get more frequent or intense headaches.
- You feel restless, and your body seems to be constantly on the move.
- You often feel rushed, irritable, and angry.
- You over-eat or under-eat.

Anxiety's flames can hypnotize and trick you into believing you can see the future. You really start to believe that if you keep vigilant and anticipate every aspect of the road ahead, you will never have to suffer negative consequences. You have it all mapped out, you have the equipment, you have even rested for it — you have it covered.

This, of course, is an illusion. No matter how hard you prepare, there are bound to be unexpected turns in the road of life — for the good as much as the bad — and this uncertainty fuels your Fireball of Anxiety.

Mental Workout Routine

Use the space below to make a note of the features of your own Fireball of Anxiety. For example, does it interfere with your sleep, or how much you concentrate at work? Does it leave you with bowel or other physical issues?

If you do not suffer from anxiety, think of someone you know who seems to suffer from it. Make a note of how you recognize the Fireball in them.

The features of your own anxiety (or someone else's)

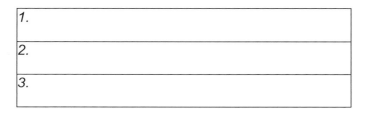

For 3 bonus points — *Make a note of three specific examples of how your anxiety (or someone else's) has impacted your life*

1.
2.
3.

Subtotal of bonus points so far: _____

An Elevated Baseline

Imagine if you were told that a group of hoodlums were outside, getting ready to storm your house to attack. That sense of terror, those dilated pupils, the raised blood pressure, and the pumping heart, are all signs that you are readying yourself for the imminent danger. For now, that is the highest priority. You are in no state to concentrate at work, or at school, and responding lovingly to your partner or kids is the last thing on your mind.

Imagine this heightened state continues for hours, days, or weeks. You will soon become depleted. Your performance at work, at school, and at home will start to deteriorate, and you won't be the best person to be around.

This is the Fireball of Anxiety. Your baseline is constantly elevated, and you are ready to pop at any moment. The clang of a dropped spoon, the slam of a door, the grimace on a person's face, will all set your heart pounding and your mind racing before you have had a moment to think. You are not designed to live in such a state of constant alertness, and yet this is the reality for millions of people in the United States and beyond.

The Anxious Brain

When the Fireball of Anxiety takes hold, your sympathetic nervous system works overtime with no extra pay. Your amygdala (the brain's alarm system) wakes up and it sounds the alarm, alerting you to a clear and present danger, even though your prefrontal cortex insists there is no such thing.

Sort of like that annoying youngest child whose parents have given up silencing, the amygdala's scream is the loudest, so we ignore the common sense of the "first child" prefrontal cortex and respond to the amygdala "youngest child" as if there really is an imminent threat.

What do you do in the face of imminent danger? You prepare to fight or flee. As we saw earlier in this Survival Guide, your sympathetic nervous system kicks in, and, fueled by adrenalin, your heart pumps faster, you begin to sweat, your pupils dilate, your blood pressure increases, and cortisol (the stress hormone) is produced. If you remain in this stressed state, your brain can actually change, making you more prone to a wide range of physical and mental health issues.

Research indicates that long periods of high cortisol levels can cause inhibited thyroid functioning, decreased bone density, increased abdominal fat, and higher blood pressure. It is also well known that the Fireball of Anxiety can cause all sorts of gastrointestinal problems; many of my clients report feeling their anxiety in this area of their body.

The Panic Room

A panic room is supposed to be a safe space, a refuge in the event of an attack. And yet, during a panic attack, it feels as if your body has become a war zone.

Your anxiety becomes so bad that you cannot breathe, your head spins, your limbs buzz with energy, you sweat like a pig, and believe you are going to die. You are sure that you have something physically wrong with you (perhaps your heart or lungs), but doctors find nothing physically amiss. Without a diagnosis or explanation, you begin to

- avoid things because you are terrified that the panic attacks could come on at any moment;
- become overly dependent on someone for things you once could do alone;
- become isolated, physically and emotionally.

Mental Workout Routine

Use the space below to make a note of your own experiences of a panic attack and how you felt during it.

If you have never experienced a panic attack, think of a time when you have witnessed one. Use the space below to make a note of what you witnessed, and what you imagine they felt.

For 3 bonus points — *Make a note of three specific examples of how your panic attacks (or someone else's) have impacted your life.*

1.
2.
3.

Subtotal of bonus points so far: _____

Panic and Anxiety, not Fear

Don't let the Fireball of Anxiety blind you so you end up confusing anxiety with a healthy measure of fear. Fear is part of the spectrum of emotions discussed in Chapters 1 and 2 of this Survival Guide, and you will recall that our emotions tell us important things. Fear alerts us to real dangers and motivates a proportionate response.

> For example, you fear the glowing stovetop and respond proportionately by keeping your hand away from it. You do not scream in horror and forever avoid the kitchen (and all kitchen appliances).

Anxiety is not a healthy level of fear. Anxiety is a disproportionate anticipation of threats that may never come to fruition. Our anxiety serves no purpose, and it sometimes leaves us less able to respond to the actual dangers that are right in front of us. We need a healthy dose of fear, but we do not need anxiety.

Mental Workout Routine

Carry out a quick review of the answers you gave above, identifying three specific examples of your own anxiety (or the anxiety of someone you know). Now, having read about the difference between fear and anxiety, which did you identify?

If you identified examples of fear, use the space below to replace them with three new examples of your experiences of anxiety (or anxiety you have witnessed in someone else).

1.
2.
3.

Panic and Anxiety, not Stress

When we refer to anxiety, we don't mean stress. Stress is typically caused by an external trigger, such as
- incessant demands from an abusive partner;
- a business merger that was poorly planned by the leadership team; or
- mismanagement of your workplace by incompetent leaders.

On the other hand, the Fireball of Anxiety can be ignited, and continue to burn, without any external trigger. We are consumed by constant worry even when there isn't anything to worry about; for example:
- You are consumed with anxious thoughts about the next meet-up with your extended family, even though they are always loving and supportive.

- You are point-blank going to avoid any chitchat in the playground with any of the other parents because you are shaking and flushed-cheek at the mere thought of it.
- You turn down a job opportunity because you can feel your legs shaking at the mere thought of it (even though you have been told by countless colleagues that you are more than qualified for it).

The Fireball's Trail of Destruction

The Fireball of Anxiety can leave a trail of destruction in your working life, your school life, or your home life. It can severely impact your ability to function at even the most basic level, and it can threaten relationships with your colleagues, friends, and family.

- With an estimated 284 million people affected by anxiety worldwide, there is a huge economic cost due to loss of productivity, healthcare costs, and other indirect costs. In the United States alone, some estimate the annual cost of anxiety to be between $42.3 billion and $46.6 billion (AJMC).
- The stigma of anxiety means that many people who need help do not seek help, or get the help they need. Unlike many physical illnesses, people who have anxiety are sometimes labeled "overthinkers," "excessive worriers," or "high maintenance."
- The World Health Organization estimates that mental health conditions such as anxiety (and depression) cost the world $1 trillion a year.
- Research suggests that parents who suffer from anxiety (without the appropriate help) can have a significant impact on the mental and physical well-being of their children. Mental health struggles of a caregiver during the first eighteen years of a child's life is considered to be one example of an adverse

childhood experience, and the higher the number of Adverse Childhood Experiences (ACEs) for a child, the greater the likelihood of impairments to a person's mental and physical well-being in adulthood. For example, an increased risk of heart disease, cancer, and strokes.

Help Beyond the Labels

Trying to draw a clear line between "anxiety" and "no anxiety" can be like drawing a line between one flame and the next. As a result, we need to exercise caution when it comes to diagnostic labels and anxiety. When professionals adhere too rigidly to diagnostic labels, they run the risk of adopting such a narrow interpretation of a person's behavior, thoughts, and emotions that they fail to identify the anxiety, leaving that person to wander the wilderness alone. As we will see, this risk increases if you are male labeled, and this risk also increases when the male label intersects with your identity beyond the blue of the male label (for example, due to the racism, transphobia, biphobia, or homophobia of the diagnosing healthcare professional).

Nevertheless, some people find the certainty of labels comforting, and so, for completeness here are some of the diagnostic labels that are attached to the Fireball of Anxiety:

Generalized Anxiety Disorder (GAD)
This is disproportionate worry, for at least six months, that generalizes across a number of different aspects of a person's life; for example, your disproportionate worries are not confined to your relationship with your partner, or your boss at work. The disproportionate worry spills out across your life, and it is extremely hard to manage.

Panic Disorder
As you saw above, panic attacks are debilitating, and a panic disorder is characterized by a number of sudden panic attacks where you feel like you cannot breathe, and you end up sweaty or dizzy.

Phobia-Related Disorders
If you are petrified every time you see someone on your doorstep with a red sweater, that would be a classified as a phobia because it is specific; it is a phobia of people in red sweaters. Phobias are intense, disproportionate fears about a specific object or situation.

Phobia-related disorders include:

Social Anxiety Disorder
An intense, disproportionate fear of social situations.

Agoraphobia
An intense, disproportionate fear of public or open spaces.

* * *

Formal Assessment Tools
Some professionals use more formal ways to assess Anxiety, and two examples are Beck's Anxiety Inventory, and GAD 7 Anxiety Test Questionnaire. For the people who prefer a formal assessment as much as a label, you can find these online:

- Beck's Anxiety Inventory — NCS Pearson Inc. owns the copyright the Beck's Depression Inventory
- GAD 7 Anxiety Test Questionnaire — Pfizer Inc. owns the copyright to GAD 7.

As we saw in Chapter 2, there is a risk that these Formal Assessment Tools might leave the Fireball of Anxiety burning beneath the surface, and the last thing we want to do is give you a "false negative," leaving you without the help you need. This risk is increased when we consider the Fireball of Anxiety and the male label.

* * *

Anxiety and the Male Label

Every year 40 million people in the US are engulfed in the Fireball of Anxiety. Though people of all genders are affected by anxiety, some claim anxiety is not a threat if you have been given the male label, as if this label were made of asbestos, or protected you with a magical, fireproof force field. The sad reality is that the Fireball is just as much a threat regardless of the sex label you have been given.

The Hidden Embers of Underreported Cases

As with depression, there is likely to be hidden embers of underreported anxiety in the male labeled thanks to societal and cultural conditioning, including:

- We expect the male labeled to be silent and strong, and so the male labeled should not admit to vulnerabilities, including anxious thoughts and feelings. Thus, shame silences you.
- The male labeled are expected to focus outwards, on external gain and power, not inwards, on emotions and thoughts. As a result, they may be unaware that what they experience is anxiety.
- The male labeled are expected to remain independent, and so to seek help is an admission of defeat. As a result, fewer male labeled are likely to access mental healthcare for anxiety, and so the

myth continues that the male labeled are somehow untouched by the Fireball.

- Due to structural inequality, the problem of a lack of access to mental healthcare is compounded when we consider how the male label intersects with a person's identity (for example, their racial or ethnic identity, true gender identity, or sexuality).

As the United States is a patriarchal society, this conditioning influences the dominant view of emotions. The preferred approach (by many with power or authority) is to focus outwards, on achievement and power. Anxiety is one of those inconvenient truths that people would rather not hear about.

As a result of this conditioning, we don't expect the male labeled to have emotions or vulnerabilities, and if we do witness them, this conflicts with our expectations. Cognitive dissonance requires us to ignore inconsistencies between our expectations of the male labeled and the reality. As a result, we expect to see more anger and aggression from the male labeled, and less emotional distress, including anxiety.

Professionals who are supposed to help the male labeled can end up pathologizing their behavior. A healthcare professional's interpretation of a person's behavior is not value-free, and we saw in Chapters 1 and 2 that there is a higher rate of diagnosis of the male labeled when it comes to externalizing disorders. Some argue that, due to the racism, transphobia, biphobia, or homophobia of the diagnosing healthcare professional, this issue is compounded when we consider a person's identity beyond the blue of their male label.

Mental Workout Routine

And you? When it comes to your experiences of anxiety, are you aware of this sort of conditioning attached to the male label? Or have you witnessed it in others?

Consider also whether this conditioning has arisen regarding the intersection of the male label and your identity (for example, your racial or ethnic identity, true gender identity, or sexuality). For example, have you experienced (or witnessed) any racism, transphobia, biphobia, or homophobia of a healthcare professional?
In the space below, make a note of three examples where you have witnessed this.

Do you think this has had an impact on your anxiety (or the anxiety you have witnessed in others)?

In the space below, make a note of three thoughts about this.

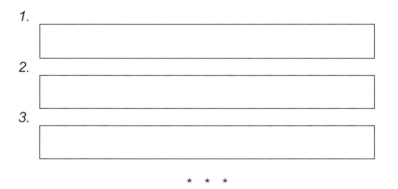

1.

2.

3.

* * *

Survival Tools Extinguish the Fireball

As you saw in Chapters 1 and 2, you have Survival Tools to extinguish your anxiety. However, if left unchecked, the Fireball will make your tools too hot to handle.

<u>Your Action Pack</u> (your behavior) — As your fears grow out of all proportion, the Fireball takes hold of your Action Pack, and you find yourself doing less of the things that you used to enjoy.

<u>Your Head Gear</u> (your thoughts) — The less you do, the faultier your Head Gear, and the more disproportionate are your fears. If you do less, you fear more of the world because you receive less evidence that it is a place of safety and contentment. Instead, your anxious thoughts lead you to believe you are more vulnerable than you really are. As your thoughts are short-circuited by anxiety, your Flashlight starts to dim.

<u>Your Flashlight</u> (your emotions) — The faultier your Head Gear, the more anxious your thoughts, and so your Flashlight dims and burns out. You simply cannot do it anymore. What might have once lit the way to greater adventures just leaves you feeling exhausted.

And so, the cycle of anxiety continues.

Figure 20 - The Anxiety Cycle

But it does not have to be this way. As we saw in Chapters 1 and 2, the more familiar you are with your Survival Tools, the easier it will be to use them to break free of the anxiety cycle. Let's look at how to use each Survival Tool to do so.

* * *

Survival Tool #1 — Action Pack (Behavior)

Old, New, and Borrowed, to Get You Beyond the Blue

You can break the anxiety cycle by engaging in actions that once made you feel competent and safe (the old), or you can create new experiences from your own brainstorming (the new), or from ideas that are borrowed from others (the borrowed).

Mental Workout Routine

Use the space set out below to answer these questions to identify the components to your Action Pack. Try to gather as many examples as possible, so your Action Pack is varied and plentiful.

What has made you feel calm and contented in the past? What is likely to again? What ideas do you have from other people to create this calm and contented state?

Were there any particular people in your life who made you feel safe and secure, or peaceful and relaxed? Who is likely to again? What ideas do you have from other people to create this safe, secure, peaceful, and relaxed state?

What activities have opened doors of hope in your mind that life can be settled and manageable? What is likely to again? What ideas do you have from other people to create hope that life can be settled and manageable?

What has left your feet solidly placed on the ground, with a sense of presence? What is likely to again? What ideas do you have from other people to create this sense of solid presence?

Lighten the Load of Your Action Pack

Don't overload your backpack with activities in which you will never engage. Shortlist the above selection by making sure they pass at least one of these tests:

1.   *The Test of Mastery* – Do the actions on your list develop a sense of mastery?

2.   *The Test of Opposite Attraction* – Try to ensure that the actions on your list evoke the opposite emotion to anxiety. For example, if the Fireball leaves you feeling frazzled, on edge, and with your mind racing, what can you do to feel calm and centered?

3.   *The Test of Appreciation* – Do the actions on your list make you appreciate what you have?

Mental Workout Routine

Create a short list of the components to your Action Pack that pass either the Test of Mastery, the Test of Opposite Attraction, or the Test of Appreciation

```
┌─────────────────────────────────────────┐
│                                          │
│                                          │
│                                          │
│                                          │
└─────────────────────────────────────────┘
```

A SMART Action Pack

As you saw earlier in this Survival Guide, you need to use the SMART approach to plan how and when you are going to engage in the actions you have packed.

S is for Specific — For example, you might find that physical exercise has helped burn off some of your anxiety in the past. But what does this entail? Are you going to go to a gym, run around the block, or rejoin your local soccer team?

M is for Measurable — For example, are you going to go to the gym twice or three times a week?

A is for Achievable — For example, are you a member of a gym that is nearby and accessible?

R is for Realistic — For example, when was the last time you went to the gym? If you have never set foot in one, the idea of doing this sounds unrealistic, so perhaps you might first try a few light workouts at home.

T is for Time-bound — For example, exactly when are you going to start going to the gym, on what days, and at what time?

Mental Workout Routine

Choose at least three components to your Action Pack and use the blank grid below (Figure 21) to assess whether each item is SMART.

If it is not SMART, what do you need to change to make it a SMART Action?

Don't forget to also use the blank schedule below (Figure 22) to make each component to your Action Pack Time-bound.

Item from your Action Pack	Specific ?	Measur-able?	Achiev-able?	Realistic ?	Time-Bound? Use the Action Planner below to create a schedule for each SMART Action item
1					
2					
3					

Figure 21 - How to Make Your Action Pack SMART

To make each Action item Time-bound -

Item from your Action Pack	Time	Day, and frequency	Intensity
1			
2			
3			

Figure 22 - How to Make Your Action Pack Time-bound

The Illusion of Safety Behavior

Some of your actions add fuel to the Fireball of Anxiety, and one example is to engage in *safety behavior*. Set out below are examples, with the safety behavior highlighted in italics.

- If you get anxious around other people and
    - You attend social gatherings
        - *but you speak quietly*, or
    - You attend social gatherings
        - *but you don't say anything*, or
    - You attend social gatherings
        - *but you leave early,* or
    - *You avoid social gatherings altogether.*

You wrap yourself in knots trying to engage in safety behavior, hoping it will keep you safe, but you have in fact wrapped yourself in something that is as flame-resistant as a silk kimono doused in lighter fluid. Your safety behavior thus adds fuel to the Fireball of Anxiety in the following ways:

- When you *speak quietly* at a social gathering, people can't really hear you, so you start to believe you really should fear social gatherings because these are events where you are embarrassed by everyone saying "Wha*t?"*, "Say it again," or just outright ignoring you.

- When you attend the social gathering and *remain silent*, everyone thinks you are socially stilted, and they start to avoid you, only proving your fear that you cannot handle these sorts of situations.

- When you *leave early*, you miss the really fun bits of the evening when everyone relaxes, and conversations and jokes flow freely. You denied yourself the opportunity to understand you are not alone when it comes to nervousness over social gatherings.

- When you *avoided the social gatherings altogether,* you denied yourself the experience of how nerves peak, and then subside, making way for, dare I say it, fun!

Here are more examples of safety behavior that will simply add fuel to the Fireball of Anxiety:

- *You try to avoid all risks, for example, by overpreparing.*
- *You turn up to an event extra early (just in case!).*
- *You work so hard that you try not to make any mistakes.*
- *You make to-do lists for most occasions.*
- *You avoid situations where you do not know everything about who will be there and what will happen.*
- *You incessantly seek reassurances from others.*

Mental Workout Routine

Using the space set out below, make a note of your own thoughts about safety behavior. Have you engaged in safety behavior, or witnessed it in others?

> [blank box]

For 3 bonus points - List three examples of safety behavior that you have engaged in, or that you have witnessed in others.

1.

> [blank box]

2.

> [blank box]

3.

[ ]

Subtotal of bonus points so far: _____

Safety behavior is reinforced by a set of unhelpful and unrealistic rules about how life should or must be. For example:

- Uncertainty and ambiguity are dangerous.
- I cannot make any mistakes.
- I cannot admit to being wrong.
- I have to know everything to be safe.
- I should not take any risks.

Mental Workout Routine

Using the space set out below, make a note of some of the rules that keep you trapped in safety behavior. If you do not think this applies to you, does it apply to anyone you know? If so, hazard a guess about the rules that trap them in their own safety behavior.

[ ]

How to Give Up Your Safety Behavior

Avoid Avoidance

Most safety behavior is predicated on avoidance; the more you avoid what makes you anxious, the more (you believe) you will remain safe from the feared catastrophe.

But in truth, avoidance only adds more fuel to the Fireball of Anxiety; the more you avoid, the less you learn about how you can handle situations, and how illusory the flames of the Fireball really are.

Here are some examples of how you can let go of your safety behavior. In short, this is how you can avoid avoidance, or, in other words, expose yourself to what fuels your anxiety.

Avoid Avoidance Example #1 — Attend that social event rather than killing off a family member

I am not really talking about homicide; no aunts, uncles, or other family members were harmed in the writing of this Survival Guide. I just mean you do not need to justify your absence from the social event by lying that a family member died. By attending that social event, you are truthful with your friends; you learn the subtle art of small talk; you learn how to breathe through those anxious feelings in the pit of your stomach; and you experience the peak of anxiety, and then how it subsides.

Avoid Avoidance Example #2 — Admit to your friend that you do need help

Safety behavior can include a pretense that everything in life is hunky-dory. When you strut around like a flamboyant peacock, emitting so much confidence it smacks of arrogance, you repel everyone. You also cheat yourself of deeper connections, where other people can feel comfortable enough to admit their own insecurities. Drop the act and share your real, raw experiences of struggles and sweat.

Avoid Avoidance Example #3 — If you avoid, you don't listen, and if you don't listen, you don't learn

Haruki Murakami once wrote, "And people who don't think are the ones who don't listen to others." If you don't drop your safety behavior, if you don't stop avoiding, you will deny yourself the chance to listen to others. And when you listen to others, you learn. You may learn that the world is not such a scary place, and other people are not such towering threats of intimidation. We are all pretty much trying to get by, and you might see that others are a little nervous too.

Avoid Avoidance Example #4 — Present at that next work conference

This will show you that you can string together more than one coherent sentence without collapsing into your boss's lap. If you allow yourself time as you give your presentation, and you take those slow, calming, inward breaths with a longer outward breath, you will give yourself the opportunity to survey the room. And you might just see smiling, nodding heads willing you to succeed.

Avoid Avoidance Example #5 — Arrange that meeting with the school principal, damn it!

You pretty much got away with your avoidance during your pre-children days, but your safety behavior of avoidance is now starting to impact your children's education. There is a teacher who is clearly not doing their job properly, so you need to raise this with the school principal, but your anxiety leaves you wanting to vomit at the thought of such a meeting.

You know you would do anything for your children, even the middle one (you know, the one who stands at the fridge, scooping sauce out of the jar with their bare hands), so you have no choice but to avoid avoidance, drop the safety behavior, and arrange that meeting with the school principal.

Mental Workout Routine

Using the space set out below, make a note of any examples of avoiding avoidance that appeal to you.

Plan for Exposure

Think of exposure as a method of desensitizing the brain to what you fear (and to what you should not fear because there is no clear and present danger). Ideally, exposure should be carried out with a trained professional, so this section is just designed to give you a flavor of what is involved.

Before you can avoid avoidance, or, in other words, expose yourself to what fuels your anxiety, you need to create a plan.

Mental Workout Routine

*Think of a future event that is likely to trigger your anxiety (we will call this the **triggering event**). You can choose one of the following examples, or you come up with your own:*
- *presenting at a meeting or in class*
- *attending a social event you would rather avoid*

- *engaging in conversation with your work colleagues or neighbors*

*Use the space below to make a note of your **triggering event**.*

No doubt when you anticipate this **triggering event**, you describe it in your mind using words such as "terrible," "awful," or "a catastrophe."

Avoiding avoidance, or *exposure*, is a strategy to teach your brain that what is disproportionately feared and labeled as "terrible," "awful," or "a catastrophe," is far from that.

Through exposure, your brain learns that, at the least, it is bad, but it is not unbearable. Better still, if you stay with it, your brain will learn that the anxiety builds up, peaks, and then subsides, as you continue to expose yourself to what you disproportionately fear.

Remember how emotions are like light waves that build, peak, and then subside? (Figure 23)

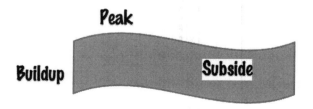

Figure 23 - The Light Waves of Your Emotions

Instead of the catastrophic language "It will be terrible or awful," say, "It might be bad, or uncomfortable, or annoying, but it is rarely terrible, awful, or a catastrophe." The way you label something makes a big difference when it comes to how you feel about it, and what you do (or don't do) in response.

Remember the nature of anxiety *versus* healthy fear?

> Healthy fear *is* proportionate. So, you should fear putting your hand on the glowing stovetop, and continue to avoid doing so.
>
> Anxiety is *not* proportionate because there is no real danger involved with the school or work meeting, or a dinner with your friends. So, you should try to avoid avoidance of those things (unless one of those friends is a serial murderer, and they know you know, and they are eyeing the steak knives with murderous intent).

When you expose yourself to the things that evoke your anxiety, you create new neural pathways. You will have a new understanding of your capabilities when you give that presentation with everyone watching you (and you do not sh*t your pants).

Here are five steps to slowly and safely plan for exposure.

Step 1. Create a Scale of Distress

Create a scale of distress (referred to as a "subjective unit of distress" or SUD), where you rate the distress level of different activities or events where:

A SUD of 0 = no distress at all, because all is hunky dory. Lucky you.

A SUD of 100 = the worst distress you could imagine. Ugh.

But what about all those numbers in between 0 and 100? What sort of activities or events would be a 10, 20, 30, 40, 50, 60, 70, 80 and 90 on your scale of distress?

You also need to add to that scale the **triggering event** you identified above. Is that a 40, 50, 60, 80, or even 90 out of 100?

Note that I asked about *your* scale of distress. This isn't about what you *should* feel or think, this is all about your *actual* level of distress. It's okay, it is only between the two of us, so no one needs to know that the thought of talking to your father-in-law is a sh*t-your-pants level 80 out of 100.

Example
Kwame is really keen to improve their relationships at work, and they hope that this might improve their career prospects. Kwame gets really anxious when they have to interact with their colleagues, so Kwame identified this as their triggering event. As a result, Kwame wishes to tackle the safety behavior of avoiding colleagues at work.

Kwame created their own scale of distress with the following SUDs:
    10 = Walking past their junior colleagues and having to smile a nonverbal *hello*
    20 = Saying "Hello" to their junior colleagues at the water cooler
    30 = Engaging in a light conversation with their junior colleagues
    40 = Walking past their senior colleagues and having to smile a nonverbal *hello*

50 = Saying "Hello" to their senior colleagues at the water cooler

60 = Engaging in a light conversation with their senior colleagues

70 = Agreeing to an after-work dinner with their junior colleagues

80 = Agreeing to an after-work dinner with their senior colleagues

90 = Passing out at a work dinner due to a panic attack

100 = Getting fired

Mental Workout Routine

*Identify the **triggering event** you wish to work on. This could be the same one as you identified in the previous section, or a new one.*

Create your own SUD scale

0 =
10 =
20 =
30 =
40 =
50 =
60 =
70 =
80 =
90 =
100 =

*Identify the SUD of your **triggering event***

SUD =

Step 2. Choose the Exposure

The next stage of the process can involve either one of two following options:

- You can *imagine* each of the following steps.
- You can engage *in* each step in *real life*.

Usually it is best to *imagine* each step of the exposure process first. Only when you can imagine each step, and you do not experience any anxiety while doing so, can you engage in exposure in *real life*.

To choose the exposure, start with an activity or event that is low on the SUD scale (for example, start with an SUD of 10), and work slowly up.

Example
Kwame decided to see how it went with SUD 10 (walking past their junior colleagues and having to smile a nonverbal *hello*).

Kwame should not jump to the next SUD level (for example, SUD 20 on the scale by saying "Hello" to their junior colleagues at the water cooler) until they review their previous exposure experience and can engage in it with no or little distress.

Mental Workout Routine

Identify the first exposure to try

Exposure =
SUD =

Step 3. Before the Exposure Exercise

Identify a self-referencing belief that might be helpful for you to carry during the exposure. For example, Kwame chose the self-referencing belief, *I am strong and capable.*

Mental Workout Routine

Self-Referencing Belief =

Step 4. During the Exposure Exercise

When you carry out the exposure, do not get put off by any peak in anxiety. Just notice it and stay with it, as if you are surfing the light wave of emotion. If you abort the mission too soon, your brain won't have a chance to learn a new experience (the new experience of tolerating this peak in anxiety, and experiencing the emotion subside).

As you ride the light wave of emotion, you might need to make use of your breathing apparatus to ground yourself in the present moment. Following these steps will help:

1. Notice each breath as it comes in through your nostrils and out through your lips. What is the temperature as the breath comes in through your nostrils? Is it cooler compared with the breath that goes out through your lips?

2. Notice what the slight pause is like between your inward breath and your outward breath.

3. Try to breathe into your diaphragm rather than your chest. You can make sure you are doing this by placing

a hand gently over the space at the top of your belly, just beneath your rib cage.

4. If your mind wanders, refocus on your breath by imagining a ribbon (of your chosen color) going in through your nostrils, down into your body, and then out through your lips.

5. Try to double the length of your outward breath compared with your inward breath (for example, two seconds in, four seconds out).
Alternatively, try square breathing: Two seconds for your inward breath, hold for two seconds, two seconds for your outward breath, hold for two seconds, and then continue to repeat this process of perfect symmetry.

Continue to ride the light wave of your emotion, and you will see how your anxiety starts to subside. At that moment your brain has learned a new way of being; you have discovered that, like Newton theorized about gravity, what goes up must come down. The anxiety peaks, then subsides.

Step 5. After the Exposure Exercise

After the exposure exercise, identify the SUD level for that activity or event you focused on. Hopefully you will see that the SUD level has decreased compared to the level during the exposure exercise.

Reflect on how the exercise went, including whether you learned anything about yourself or the experience.

When you experience no distress with this particular activity or event, try the next activity or event one level up on the SUD scale.

Example

After Kwame successfully imagined, and then tried in real life, walking past their junior colleagues and having to smile a nonverbal *hello,* they found that the SUD was at 0.

When they reflected on the exercise, Kwame realized they were making assumptions about their colleagues, who were friendlier than Kwame had believed them to be.

As a result, Kwame successfully started saying "Hello" to their junior colleagues, and engaging in light conversation, which gave them more confidence to smile a nonverbal *hello* to their senior colleagues.

Mental Workout Routine

Identify the SUD after the Exposure exercise

SUD =

Reflect on how the exercise went:

Identify the next Exposure to try

Exposure =
SUD =

Still Not Convinced About Giving up Your Safety Behavior?

If you are still not convinced about giving up on your safety behavior, consider these five final points:

1.   Penicillin, the Pacemaker, and the Slinky

One part of safety behavior is about keeping yourself safe from mistakes; you assume that the pain of making a mistake will be so great that it is better to avoid mistakes altogether. But is this true?

What do penicillin, the pacemaker, and the Slinky all have in common? They were created because of mistakes. So, imagine how unhealthy and dull life would be if we all engaged in safety behavior and never allowed for mistakes. Why on earth would you want to miss out on the messy fun (and learning experience) of a few mistakes every now and then?

2.   The Jumped-Up Jackass of Perfection

Think of the most perfect person you know. Got a mental image? My guess is that they have gleaming white teeth, a full head of hair, tanned skin, and immaculate clothes. Am I right?

And my guess is that you cannot stand that jackass. Am I right again?

Jumped-up jackasses of perfection make us feel inadequate, insecure, and about as interesting as an infomercial for mesothelioma. Why on earth would you want to be like them? There is humanity in your humility, and people want to see your slightly disheveled, half-ironed shirt with a stain on it that you blame on the baby you were feeding this morning (when the truth is that you haven't a clue where the stain came from, and you haven't fed a baby in years). Other people will let out the biggest exhale of relief when they realize that you are just as disorganized and messy as the rest of them.

3. Are You *Good Enough* to Tolerate Imperfection?

As hard as you try, you will make mistakes, and in fact, this is what you are supposed to do. This was the general approach conceptualized by psychoanalyst Donald Winnicott when he referred to "good enough" parenting. Children need to see their parents make mistakes so they can learn a healthy tolerance of imperfection and develop the ability to compromise.

4. Skydivers Make Great Muses

Imagine you were setting up an art exhibit, you had space left for just one more picture, and the choice was between
- an action shot of a skydiver the moment they launched themself from a plane; or
- a picture of a to-do list, typed up neatly and paginated.

The fact is, skydivers make great muses because they hurl themselves into the abyss of uncertainty. They challenge our natural instinct to reach out to our caregiver, and to have someone to catch us before we fall. So throw out of a plane your childish need for certainty. You are a full-fledged adult with a bank account and mortgage, so you need a bit of stomach-churning *un*certainty to remind you that you are still very much alive.

5. Cost-Benefit Analysis

When blinded by the Fireball of Anxiety, you fail to realize that by engaging in safety behavior, you are missing out on so much of life. Your anxiety gets you so caught up in

179

focusing on risks, you fail to see the benefits you're missing.

So be honest with yourself and carry out this calculation:

The costs involved with engaging in that safety behavior (*i.e.*, what are you missing out on?)

versus

The benefits involved with engaging in that safety behavior.

In this calculation, only include actual benefits, not vague claims that you might avoid a potential threat in the future. And don't short-change yourself; you need to calculate the true value of short-term *versus* long-term costs and benefits.

As we saw with depression, your Action Pack is the quickest and easiest of the three Survival Tools to use. But it alone does not always help you to break free of the anxiety cycle.

* * *

Survival Tool #2 — Head Gear (Your Thoughts)

Triggered Like an H-bomb

You have seen how your Action Pack (your behavior) can keep you trapped in the anxiety cycle as much as it can break you free. The same can be said for your Head Gear (your thought process).

Here are some examples of Head Gear faults that create sparks to reignite the Fireball of Anxiety:

- You cannot focus at work because your mind keeps drifting back to the client you must meet

180

with tomorrow, and you are sure, *absolutely sure*, you will say something that comes across as stupid or insensitive.

- On another day, you lie awake at night, trying to figure out how you can stay home instead of having to attend the upcoming weekend family gathering because you know, *you just know*, that everyone will start comparing lifestyles, salaries, and the size of everyone's house.

- And then, on another day, you know you should speak to your child's coach about their performance, but *you know* your throat will constrict and dry up and you will sound like a high-pitched, deflating balloon.

Figure 24 - The Anxiety Cycle

Is it any wonder why you cannot sleep when these thoughts make your heart pound and your head throb?

- You can get anxious about the *internal:*
  For example, you feel your fluttering heart and shortness of breath, so you believe you must be

anxious, and so there must be things you need to worry about, and… then you really become anxious

- You can get anxious about the *external:*
  For example, you believe that they are staring at you, and they know you made a mistake in your presentation at work, so they think that you are an incompetent buffoon.

Your Head Gear is misfiring so much it is triggering you like an H-bomb. So you need to fix the faults before they destroy you, your career, and your loved ones.

As Simple as A-B-C

As we've seen earlier in this Survival Guide, the ABC log is a tool used to help understand the intricate functioning (and malfunctioning) of our Head Gear. We need this log because our thought process fires so rapidly we barely notice it, let alone challenge it, even when it has completely missed the mark.

Mental Workout Routine

Use the blank ABC log set out below (see Figure 25) to record an example of when you last felt anxious. Complete columns A, B, and C for now.

If you haven't ever experienced anxiety, complete columns A, B, and C, for someone else who has.

A	B	C	D	E
Activating Event	Beliefs & Assump-tions	Conse-quence	Dispute	Evaluate

Figure 25 - ABC Log

By way of brief recap of columns A, B and C -

Column A — The Activating Event (Trigger)

The activating event (or trigger) refers to what was happening at the time of your anxiety:

- What was going on?
- Who was involved?
- Was there anything out of the ordinary about what you were doing, or what others were doing around you?

Example
Juan is a building contractor who is the kind of person you can rely on:

Juan turns up early to site meetings, after having spent the night before monitoring the weather for the next day.

Juan will also listen diligently, take copious notes, and will carry out your instructions to the letter.

In fact, Juan goes that extra mile so much that Juan's business is now running at a loss.

Juan's business partners left years ago, exasperated by Juan's incessant need to cover every base (and spend every last dollar of potential profit). Because of their desire to go over and above the instructions, overthinking every detail, and lacking the ability to trust their own judgment, Juan is even losing customers. Juan, and their business, is being consumed by the Fireball of Anxiety.

The latest Activating Event (or trigger) for Juan's anxiety was a meeting with a new client who needed a new garage built at their property. As usual, Juan diligently took notes during the meeting but started to second-guess every last detail, especially the location of the property line.

The anxiety kept Juan up all night as they searched the notes and their memory of the client meeting. Juan searched for an answer as to the location of the property line, yet the more they focused on this issue, the more they doubted other instructions of the client:

"If I get the property line wrong, I will build the garage on the neighbor's land, and then the client and the neighbor will sue me. I can't afford a lawsuit, as that would mean I would lose my home, and then my kids' lives will be ruined.

And what if I misheard other instructions from the client? Perhaps I misheard them about the finish and color they want. Perhaps I have not listened carefully to any of my clients properly. I am pretty sh*t at most *things in life, and I guess that is what the business partners thought when they left; I am a loser, a f#ckup.*

What other projects are going to go wrong, leading to lawsuit after lawsuit? I guess I am just someone who cannot listen properly, probably because I have some sort of undiagnosed ADHD, so I shouldn't be in this line of work, let alone have my own business. This is probably why I lost my business partners, and why those three clients last month chose to go with someone else. They could just sense that I was not up to this kind of work."

And the Fireball of Anxiety did not just destroy Juan's peace of mind for that night. As a result of sleeplessness, Juan could not concentrate on two other projects the following day and made silly mistakes, which added fuel to the Fireball, causing another night of helpless doubts.

The above extract demonstrates the hasty, feverish tone set by anxious thoughts, so next we will examine the Head Gear for faults.

Column B — Beliefs and Assumptions

At the time of the activating event, when the Fireball of Anxiety ignited, what were your beliefs or assumptions?

We make assumptions about how things should or should not be, or how we should have behaved or thought or felt in that moment.

We also fill the gap where we are missing knowledge, assuming, for example, what someone thinks about us.

We also carry around beliefs about ourselves, others, and the world around us. For example, *The world is unsafe*, or *Others cannot be trusted*, or *I am unlovable*.

Common Faults with your Head Gear

Your beliefs and assumptions (your Head Gear) can make you more or less vulnerable to the Fireball of Anxiety, depending on how faulty your Head Gear is.

Here is a reminder of the seven common faults that undermine your Head Gear:

1. All-or-Nothing Thinking
You forgot your lines at a marketing presentation, once, five years ago, and so your anxiety stops you from engaging in any sort of marketing for your company ever again.

2. Emotional Reasoning
You feel incompetent when you stand up to present at a work conference, so your anxiety intensifies because you believe that you really are incompetent. Slipping into the "feeling is believing" trap blinds you to the praise your colleagues are whispering about you right at this very moment.

3. Putting the Ass in Assumptions
You assume the other parents at the playground are angry with you because they leave the school just when you arrive; thus the next morning your stomach churns with anxiety because you do not want to face an angry mob. But these parents had to leave promptly the previous day because they had meetings to attend.

4. The Tyranny of the Shoulds
You believe you should score a goal at every match, and so your anxiety burns you out, making you want to quit the sport entirely.

5. Personalization
Every time your boss shuts the door to their office, you just *know* they are discussing when and how to fire you.

6. Catastrophic Thinking
Your daughter develops a fever, and you rush them to hospital.

7. Dodgy Filter, Overgeneralizations, and Labeling
You never remember any of your performance reviews at work, other than the less than favorable one of two years ago. As a result, your anxiety causes you to have a panic attack every time you think of your next review.

Example

Here are the faults in Juan's Head Gear:
- *Catastrophic Thinking* — There are numerous examples, not least of which include, *"the client and the neighbor will sue me,"* and *"my kids' lives will be ruined."*
- *Labeling* — *"I am a loser, a f#ckup"* is an example.
- *Dodgy Filter* — *"And perhaps I have not listened carefully to any of my clients properly. I am pretty sh*t at most things in life"* is an example. Juan is ignoring the times they have done well at work, and they are taking one moment of doubt to fuel the Fireball of Anxiety.
- *Personalization* - *"If I get the property line wrong"* is an example. It isn't just down to Juan to accurately delineate the property line.

To complete column B of the ABC log, we also need to rate how firmly Juan holds onto their beliefs. To do this, we use a scale of 1 to 7, where
1 = Juan doesn't really believe it, and
7 = Juan wholeheartedly believes it.

This will serve as a baseline when Juan disputes and re-evaluates those beliefs in columns D and E of the ABC log. For example, Juan quite strongly believes that they are a loser because they rate this at 6 out of 7.

Column C — Consequences (Emotional and Behavioral)

As a result of the activating event you noted in column A, and the beliefs and assumptions you noted in column B

- How do you feel? This is what we mean by the emotional consequences. If you feel anxious, how would you rate that on a scale of 0 to 10, where
    - 0 = no anxiety at all, and
    - 10 = intense anxiety.

- What did you do? For example, did you engage in more safety behavior, such as avoidance or over preparedness?

Example
Juan felt intense anxiety, at a rating of 9 out of 10, and this was not helped by the lack of sleep.

In addition, because Juan could not sleep, they made mistakes on other work projects in the days that followed. Juan also ended up contacting their client (who needed the garage built) and wasting the client's time by checking every single detail of that meeting. This alienated the client so much that they withdrew their business.

Juan also avoided taking on more work because they mistakenly believed they were a *"f#ck up."* As we have seen previously, safety behavior can only add more fuel to the Fireball of Anxiety.

Column D — Disputing or Correcting Beliefs and Assumptions

To break the anxiety cycle, you need to fix any faults in your Head Gear.

You will recall, there are seven common faults that can undermine your Head Gear, and set out below is a quick recap of how to fix each one.

1. All-or-Nothing Thinking
Think in terms of shades of grey, and find a middle ground.

2. Emotional Reasoning
Balance your emotions with other sources of information, including logic, an analysis of all the facts, and proportionality. Remember, the hallmark of anxiety is that the fear is out of proportion to the threat.

3. Putting the Ass in Assumptions
To stop making assumptions, check that you have all the facts, and stop trying to mind read.

4. The Tyranny of the Shoulds
Try replacing your shoulds and musts with a preference, "I would like," or "I would prefer."

5. Personalization
Who or what else is involved? It ain't all about you (which can be a relief).

6. Catastrophic Thinking
Scale down your language, as few things are catastrophic, urgent, or even imperative.

7. Dodgy Filter, Overgeneralizations, and Labeling

Adopt a balanced approach by incorporating the good and bad in an evaluation, and resist the overgeneralization of a label. Be specific.

Mental Workout Routine

Turn again to the blank ABC log (see Figure 25). Previously, you filled out columns A, B, and C for when you were last anxious or, if you hadn't experienced anxiety, you were supposed to complete those columns for someone else who had experienced anxiety.

Now have a go at filling out column D; try to fix any faulty Head Gear you have identified in column B. Note if there were any examples of

- *all-or-nothing thinking;*
- *emotional reasoning;*
- *putting the ass in assumptions;*
- *the tyranny of the shoulds;*
- *personalization;*
- *catastrophic thinking;*
- *dodgy filter, overgeneralizations, and labeling.*

Example

Catastrophic Thinking

- Juan could check whether they have all the relevant information instead of jumping to catastrophic conclusions. No one is currently suing Juan, and the likelihood of getting to that point seems pretty low. It is even more a stretch of the imagination that this would then also lead to Juan's kids having ruined lives.

- Anxiety is fueled by this forward-looking perspective and an illusion that we can somehow predict that future; and if we can predict it, we can plan for it.

- The trouble with anxiety is that we are so preoccupied with a future uncertainty, we don't realize there is a great deal to focus on in the present moment.
- There might be an element of truth in Juan's self-criticisms; they are so focused on all the different paths their life could take in the future, they are not paying attention to the present moment.
- Stop worrying about the loss of future revenue, and all the icky consequences of that (for you and your family) when you have a current, paying client demanding your attention!

Labeling

- Labels are far too simplistic to reflect the true reality. Juan might have made one mistake by not listening to one piece of detail about one part of one transaction for one client, but this does not make the whole of Juan, their whole identity, a *"loser"* or a *"f#ckup."*
- If we were to define a *"f#ckup"* or*"loser,"* that would not include someone who has spent ten years generating profit in a business. As the label is so vague, we are not just looking at Juan's working life, so I guess a *"loser"* or *"f#ckup"* is not someone who married their childhood sweetheart, has been happily married for ten years, and created three beautiful children as a result.

Dodgy Filter

- Instead of filtering out all the positive feedback Juan has received from clients over the years, Juan needs to balance out the negative thoughts with a list of that positive feedback.
- When Juan completes a task, they are not allowed to criticize or doubt their decisions in that meeting without two positive or reassuring things to say about it.

- It is all about having a balanced view; not an overly optimistic, saccharine-sweet view, and not one that tastes of sh*t.
- When Juan works on their anxiety, they will realize they do not need a complete personality transplant; many clients love how attentive Juan is, so we don't want to lose this completely.
- What we are looking for is a more balanced perspective:
    - attentiveness to clients, and attention to detail, balanced with
    - an ability to draw the line and make a decision without too much client input.

Personalization
- To depersonalize the situation, Juan needs to realize that ownership of property and boundary lines is the responsibility of the client, the property owner.

Column E Is for Evaluating

Now you have had a chance to fix the faults in your Head Gear, you can re-evaluate your beliefs and emotions.

Re-evaluate Your Beliefs
Remember that in column B you identified beliefs and assumptions, and you rated the beliefs on a scale of 1 to 7?

How would you rate those original beliefs now, on a scale of 1 to 7, where
       1 = you don't really believe it, and
       7 = you wholeheartedly believe it.

For example, Juan initially held the belief that they were a "*loser*," and rated this as a 6 out of 7; after fixing the faults of their Head Gear, they re-evaluated this belief as a 3 out of 7.

In column E, you will also need to create a new, more constructive belief to replace the above-mentioned (unhelpful) belief. Try to give this new belief a rating from 1 to 7, where

> 1 = you don't really believe it, and
> 7 = you wholeheartedly believe it.

For example, Juan could try the more constructive belief, *I am a diligent and hard worker*. Juan rates this new belief a 5 out of 7.

Re-evaluate Your Emotions
Remember that in column C you recorded the original score, on a scale of 0 to 10, for your anxiety (or the anxiety of a person you know).

Now that you have used column D to fix the faults in your Head Gear, how would you rate your anxiety on a scale of 0 to 10, where

> 0 = no anxiety, and
> 10 = intense anxiety?

If you are doing this for someone else, how would you imagine their anxiety level has changed as a result of fixing the faults in their Head Gear?

The theory is that you may, eventually, see a decrease in this level of distress.

For example, after Juan challenged their beliefs and assumptions in column D, they rated their anxiety to be a much lower 4 out of 10 (when it had initially been a 9 out of 10, when recorded in column C).

You can find a completed example of the ABC log for Juan set out below in Figure 26.

Mental Workout Routine

Turn again to the blank ABC log (Figure 25). Previously, you filled out columns A, B, C, and D for when you were last anxious (or for someone you know).

Now have a go at filling out column E —

Re-evaluate Your Beliefs
Re-evaluate any beliefs and assumptions (that you identified in column B) on a scale where
        1 = you don't really believe it, and
        7 = you wholeheartedly believe it.

Create a new, more constructive belief to replace the above-mentioned (unhelpful) belief. Try to give this new belief a rating from 1 to 7, where
        1 = you don't really believe it, and
        7 = you wholeheartedly believe it.

Re-evaluate Your Emotions
Re-evaluate your anxiety (as identified in Column C) on a scale of 0 to 10, where
        0 = no anxiety, and
        10 = intense anxiety
If you are doing this for someone else, how would you imagine their anxiety level has changed as a result of fixing the faults in their Head Gear?

The theory is that you may, eventually, see a decrease in this level of distress.

Continue to monitor yourself and reflect on how you are progressing with this.

A	B	C	D	E
Activating Event	**Beliefs & Assumptions**	**Conse- quences**	**Dispute**	**Evaluate**
Example-	Example -	Example -	Example -	Example -
Meeting with a new client	1.Catastrophic thinking - For example, "the client and the neighbor will sue me," and "my kids' lives will be ruined."	Emotional consequences - Juan felt intense anxiety, at a rating of 9 out of 10	To fix catastrophic thinking: Am I missing any information?	Juan's belief that they are a "loser" reduced to 3 out of 7.
	2. Labeling - "I am a loser, a f#ckup"	Behavioral consequences - Juan avoided taking on more work	To challenge the labeling, be more specific. Also, what are the other things that make up Juan's identity?	Juan chose a more constructive belief of "I am a diligent and hard worker." Juan rated this new belief a 5 out of 7.
	3.Dodgy Filter - "I am pretty sh*t at most things in life"		To fix the dodgy filter, instead of generalizing one or two negative experiences, carry out a balanced review of the good and bad.	Juan's anxiety was rated at a lower 4 out of 10
	4.Personalization -"If I get the property line wrong"			
	Belief - "I am a loser," and rated this a 6 out of 7.		Depersonalize the promotion: There are many other reasons for this.	

Figure 26 - Completed ABC Log

195

Eight-Point Check of Your Head Gear

To become adept at using your Head Gear to break free of the anxiety cycle, you need this handy eight-point check of your beliefs and assumptions:

1. Identify the Type of Faults in Your Head Gear
Stop to consider which fault might be undermining your Head Gear, whether it is a dodgy filter, the short-circuited reasoning of emotional reasoning, or any of the other faults.

2. Prove it or Lose it
If you do not have the information to support your assumption, drop it like a hot potato fresh out of the campfire. You can only live according to the facts you know; everything else is circumspect guesswork.

3. Flex your Flexibility
If there is a fire, you are not going to stand still, hoping it will somehow extinguish itself. You need the flexibility to escape any constraint, and get the hell out of there.

And you need to flex yourself in two ways to escape the trap of inflexibility:

Firstly, you might rigidly hold onto anxiety because it is all you have ever known; you fear if you are not a constantly vigilant person, then who are you? To maintain a balanced family system, you might have been given anxiety by your caregivers who might have allocated you the role of "worrier," "stressed-out one," or "scapegoat." But you can challenge any fixed role allocated to you by stepping out of the expectations accompanying this role. For example, you could
   * go to that social event;
   * speak up when your friends next gather; or
   * take the initiative and plan the next social gathering.

196

The options are endless because you are a multidimensional and fascinating person beyond any fixed role that has ever been expected of you.

Secondly, flex your flexibility by challenging your assumptions, which can make an ASS out of U and ME. Resist making assumptions about
- yourself;
- others; and
- the world around you.

4. Watch your Language

When I work with people to help them break free of the anxiety cycle, their language often reflects a life or death level of seriousness. Air raid sirens are going off in their heads (in the form of their amygdala), planes are circling, and they swear they just saw bombs being dropped from on high.

Their language reflects this level of catastrophe but the reality is a great deal more mundane, because they forgot to send an email to their client last night, or they realized they overspent this month and they will have to postpone repayment of their credit card until next month.

No one is dying in these situations, so let's reserve the life or death language for when it is truly warranted.

5. Scale it down

To help scale down your language, use the scale of distress that you devised in the previous section (when you were planning for exposure).

Here is a quick reminder of your own SUD:

0 =
10 =
20 =
30 =
40 =
50 =
60 =
70 =
80 =
90 =
100 =

6. Phone a friend

Get some validation, get challenged, get supported, and get a sense of normality in this crazy, isolating world. We need each other to do all of this, and more. So, share your anxious thoughts, with a smile or as a joke, if you like, but share them. When you hear that others have similar random thoughts, even looping, endless thoughts of fear for a future uncertain, it can help you to feel less isolated, but it can also afford you the chance to hear how they have coped. Learn from others who have walked the same beaten path.

7. Talk to yourself

It isn't a good idea to tell those anxious thoughts to "f#ck off" for studies show that denial or repression of anxiety often leads to a magnification of that anxiety. So if you try to kick anxiety out, it is only going to return all tooled up, and it may even bring its partner, the panic attack.

Instead, reassure your anxiety with a kind, compassionate voice. It is okay to be vigilant, and this might have kept you safe in the past, so you have that part of your brain to thank for keeping you safe back then. But in the present, you can assess if the fears are disproportionate or inappropriate, and ask that part of your brain to take a break for a while. After all, if it has been working overtime to keep you safe, doesn't it need a rest?

8. Cost-Benefit Analysis

You may think that remaining vigilant by keeping these anxious thoughts somehow keeps you safe. Yes, you could avoid that one-in-a-million chance of an electric pylon falling on our head by staying at home, but at what cost?

So far in our journey, we have explored the use of your Action Pack (behavior) and Head Gear (thought process) to break the anxiety cycle. There is one final way, and that is with the aid of your Flashlight (emotions).

* * *

Survival Tool #3 – The Flashlight of Your Emotions

Remember how you used the Flashlight to break free of the depression cycle? In the same way, you can use this Survival Tool to escape the anxiety cycle.

Your emotions communicate important information, without which you are left to wander the wilderness in the dark. But to know how to use it, you need to become familiar with each of its components, so here is a quick refresher.

Component 1
The Multicolored Words of the Flashlight

The Flashlight has a full spectrum of emotion words, but why is this important?

Mental Workout Routine

Using the space below, make a note of why it is important to be familiar with the full spectrum of emotion words. Think particularly about how this might be helpful for you when it comes to your Fireball of Anxiety.

The answers are set out below. And don't cheat!

```

```

Answers

Your emotions communicate important information to yourself and others. If you are unable to articulate the actual emotion you are experiencing, you are less likely to get your needs met. For example, you may feel anxious about your partner when they don't answer your telephone calls. If you are only aware of anger or sadness, your partner is less likely to understand what you need than if you are able to articulate you are feeling fear or loneliness.

Don't look at it yet, until after you have completed the next Mental Workout Routine, but Figure 27 offers the full palette of emotions you can use to clearly, and more accurately, communicate your needs.

Remember also to name the intensity of the Emotion. You can use a scale of 0 to 10, where -
        0 = A very low, flat-lined level of intensity
        10 = An intense, psychedelic level of intensity

Mental Workout Routine

Using the space below, make a list of all the emotion words you can remember from earlier chapters in this Survival Guide.

The answers are set out below. Again, don't cheat!

Answers

Component 1
The Multicolored Words of the Flashlight

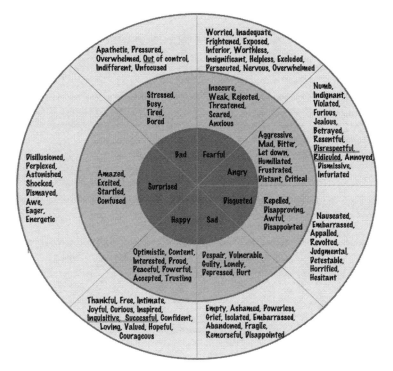

Figure 27 - The Full Spectrum of Your Emotions

Mental Workout Routine

Can you remember the sources of power for your Flashlight? Use the space below to list three.
You will find the answers set out below.

1.	
2.	
3.	

Answers

Here are some of the sources of power for your Flashlight:

- *sleep*
- *food*
- *drink*
- *drugs, prescription or otherwise*
- *exercise*
- *absence of stressful experiences over a recent period*
- *extent to which you have over/under-scheduled yourself.*

You may feel particularly anxious because you have been drinking too much coffee, or eating too much sugar, or staying up late into the night. To use your Flashlight wisely so you can survive and thrive out there in the wilderness of your life, you need to understand when your power pack might become depleted. We all have our own rhythms; some need more or less sleep, some are more or less sensitive to alcohol, and some need more or less exercise.

Mental Workout Routine

Use the grid in Figure 28 to identify your own patterns in the intensity of your anxiety. If you have not experienced anxiety yourself, think of someone who has, and use the grid to identify their patterns.
The patterns of intensity will be identified by keeping a note of

- *sleep schedules*
- *what is consumed (food, drink, drugs)*
- *any exercise*
- *accumulation of stressful experiences over a recent period*
- *how much you over/under-scheduled yourself.*

Day	Sleep Schedule	Consumption of food, drink, and drugs	Exercise	Stressful experiences?	Over/Under-scheduled?
Monday					
Tuesday					
Wednesday					
Thursday					
Friday					
Saturday					
Sunday					

Figure 28 - How to Master the Intensity of Your Flashlight

Component 3
Master the Dimmer Switch

To regulate the Flashlight, you need to master the Dimmer Switch. Anxiety often makes us feel too much, and so we need to learn how to turn the Dimmer Switch down a little.

Mental Workout Routine

To test your knowledge, use the space below to remind yourself of how you can master the Dimmer Switch.
You will find the answers set out below.

Answers

To regulate your emotions and master the Dimmer Switch, you can use grounding, breathing or visualization exercises, which will give you space to choose how to respond to your triggers, so you can cope in a healthier, less reactive way.

For example, you are overwhelmed by your partner's family who are all on their way to visit you. You are racing around trying to tidy up, and you just know that when they get there, they are going to let their kids rampage through your home and leave a mess.

You recognize the sharp increase in emotion, and you would usually scream and shout at your own family to help with the tidying, but instead:

You stimulate your five senses to ground yourself (this is the grounding exercise detailed in Chapter 2).

You engage your breathing apparatus so you can activate your ventral vagal nerve network, reducing the harmful cortisol (stress hormone) (this is the breathing exercise detailed in Chapter 2).

You activate the power pack of your imagination to visualize a calmer scene. This gives you more time to respond in a measured, and more assertive way (this is the visualization exercise detailed in Chapter 2).

If you need a reminder of each step of these exercises, review Chapter 2.

* * *

Your Shelter of Resilience

So far we have identified the Fireball of Anxiety, including how this threatens the male labeled, and we have explored how to use your three Survival Tools to break the cycle of anxiety.

You will recall that we also have a Shelter of Resilience to keep us safe during our long and winding journey through life. Sometimes the Fireball can spread rampantly, and our only option left is to seek refuge behind these fireproof walls.

Let's carry out a quick review of the four walls of the Shelter of Resilience discussed in Chapter 1.

Wall One: Self-Compassion

When the Fireball of Anxiety starts to rage, we become consumed by the toxicity of our incessantly self-critical voice. The only place we have to breathe is behind the Wall of Self-Compassion.

Mental Workout Routine

Do you remember what materials we used to construct the Wall of Self-Compassion?
Using the space below, make a note of what you can remember. No cheating!

The answers are set out below.

Answers:

The Wall of Self-Compassion is constructed of:

- *Kindness to yourself*
- *A desire to see the end of suffering*
- *An acceptance that you are human, and you are bound to make mistakes*
- *A desire to learn, and a leniency, rather than a tendency to preach and punish*
- *A mindful and balanced approach to life.*

You can create this Wall of Self-Compassion with the same kind, understanding, and forgiving words that you reserve for your loved ones. So take a deep breath and then slowly exhale as you direct these words inwards:

- *I tried my best, that is all I can ever do*
- *I will work it out*
- *I can learn from this*
- *I can try a different way next time*
- *I did the best with what knowledge and resources I had at the time*
- *I will take one day at a time*

But one wall alone will not keep you safe from the flames of anxiety, so you need to make sure you have a fully constructed Shelter of Resilience. Have a look at Chapter 1 and remind yourself of what it takes to construct and maintain the other walls of the Shelter of Resilience.

*   *   *

Three Secrets about the Fireball of Anxiety

Promise you won't tell anyone? Really promise? Okay, here are three secrets about the Fireball of Anxiety.

Secret One: Some People Crave the Burn

When night descends and you can feel the bite of the cold air, the Fireball's heat may seem quite tempting. Why would we choose the darkness of uncertainty when we fear it holds future catastrophes?

We crave the burn of the Fireball because we see it as our protection from the future uncertainty we fear. Somehow, we believe, our anxiety will keep the wolves at bay so
our career will not be devoured;
our partner will not disappear; and
our children will not be hurt.

But the Fireball of Anxiety offers just an illusion of comfort and safety. The fire of your catastrophic thinking is not keeping at bay the threat of an uncertain future. Fearing a future catastrophe won't stop it, and anxiety is not the same as preparation. In fact, anxiety is the opposite; it burns down your Shelter of Resilience.

There is no way to avoid uncertainty, so warm yourself instead by embracing acceptance of that uncertainty, and seek comfort within the Four Walls of your Shelter of Resilience:
Self-Compassion
Self-Esteem
Self-Awareness through Acceptance
Self-Care.

Secret Two: Just When the Fireball Seems All-encompassing, It Disappears

As a psychotherapist, I have worked with clients who have been consumed by the Fireball of Anxiety, and then, for no apparent reason, they walk clear of the flames as if they are a phoenix rising from the ashes. As we saw with the Beast of Depression, no one can say for sure what makes depression or anxiety come and go. It is rarely one thing, and anyone who tries to make you believe otherwise is dabbling in the dark art of trickery.

But you can say for sure that you will give yourself the best chance to survive and thrive if you make use of your Survival Tools and the Shelter of Resilience.

Secret Three: The Fireball Can Be Dampened, but the Embers Often Continue to Glow

Some clients complain that they work on their anxiety and still it reignites in later years. This is to be expected. For many people, the intensity of the Fireball decreases, so much that you cannot see any flames, but for others, embers will always glow in the pit of their stomach, just waiting to reignite.

The idea is that the frequency of this reignition, and the intensity of the Fireball, decreases each time you work on this a little more. The more familiar and adept you are at using the Survival Tools and the Shelter of Resilience, the more likely you are to survive and thrive.

* * *

If You Are in Crisis

If you find yourself beyond the blue and your anxiety or panic attacks become so intense that you feel like you are in crisis, please seek immediate professional help. Turn to Appendix Crisis for further information.

* * *

Survive and Thrive Recap

In this chapter, you

- learned how to identify the Fireball of Anxiety;
- witnessed the trail of destruction left by this Fireball;
- explored the myths surrounding anxiety and the male label, including the intersection of the male label with your racial or ethnic identity, true gender identity, or sexuality;
- learned how to use the three Survival Tools to break free of the anxiety cycle; and
- reminded yourself of the Four Walls of your Shelter of Resilience.

We need to let our imagination go beyond the blue of the male label. If we can accept that the male labeled do suffer from anxiety, and we reduce the structural obstacles to accessible mental healthcare, this will lead to a safer and healthier society for all, before we are lost beyond the blue of anxiety.

CHAPTER 4

BEYOND THE BLUE OF YOUR RELATIONSHIP CONFLICT AND ANGER

'm going to have a Sophia from *The Golden Girls* moment, but instead of picturing *"Sicily, 1922...,"* picture this:

> *Your kid's school has only just contacted you to say that everyone needs to wear orange the next day. You have nothing orange for your kids because it makes their complexion look like their kidneys are failing.*
>
> *You quickly buy the last orange t-shirt at your local Target, and just as you start to hate yourself for adding to the consumerism that will result in an even bigger landfill from your family home, your tire blows, and you have to wait for the tow truck. This sets you behind on a project, which leads to a hellish week at work, and every time you come home to the pressures at home, you just want to turn around and walk back out of the door.*
>
> *You can't walk out on your family, so you grab your kid and try to comfort them, but they smack you in the face with a toy, and then your significant other tells you not to wind the kid up, and then you start to question the significance of your other, and anger builds as relationship conflict gathers momentum like an impending hurricane.*

Sound a bit like your own life? Life throws the occasional spanner in the works, but when you add in the pressure of kids, finances, or even a pandemic, life with your significant other, or your friends, or your work colleagues, or family, becomes so much harder.

And then you turn on each other, picking at the smallest of faults as if they will make or break you, for example:

- You don't answer their text messages quickly enough (or at all).
- They forget to pick up your kid from practice.
- You don't pursue the promotion you spent a year talking about so you could both climb out of this financial pressure.
- They don't show your family as much kindness as you think they should.

We hurt the ones we love because they are the closest to us. Something startles you, angers you, or scares you, and your words fly out as if you cannot control them. At the time, you believe you are helpless to this impulse. But the truth is you are not helpless. In fact, there is a great deal you can do to help yourself and the travel companions in your life.

You thought it would be fun to have these travel companions; you saw life's long, winding road ahead of you, and you thought you needed people to talk to, share stories with, and laugh and eat and drink together. But lately your partner, your best friend, your brother, your work colleagues, and even your parents, have made you want to live on a remote island in the Atlantic Ocean, or in a castle, with the drawbridge up, and the crocodiles snapping in the surrounding moat.

Mental Workout Routine

Use the space set out below to list three examples of relationship conflict in your own life. This can involve the

213

same travel companion, or you can offer one example for three different travel companions.

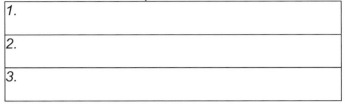

There is an important question for us to answer if we really are going to invest time and energy (and sometimes heartache) trying to resolve relationship conflict:

Do you really need your travel companions? Do you need that partner, those friends, and those family members who profess their half-baked conspiracy theories at every single damn holiday?

Is There Really Strength in Numbers?

Yes.

Short answer, but no less true. Not convinced? Okay, let's bring in the drugged-up rats.

Drugged-up Rats

Far, far away, at a university in Vancouver (Simon Fraser University, to be precise), Professor Alexander built a cage for some rats to play in. The Professor installed balls and tunnels and food, and offered the rats two water bottles,

one with water, and
one laced with drugs.

Do you know what happened? When the rats had each other for company, they chose the plain water. But when they were placed in isolation, they were tempted by the drugged water. Even more interesting, when the rats were returned to their buddies in the fun cage, their interest in the drug disappeared. Some argue this experiment contains a powerful message about the value of connection.

As mentioned earlier in this Survival Guide, human connection gives us a reason to live. It soothes us, and it confirms the edges of our personalities. We can try and deny it, and we can go it alone for a while, but eventually we will need to connect with others.

Neuroscientists have discovered that we learn more, produce more, and are generally happier when we connect with friends and family. Connecting with others develops more dimensions to our brain, and it gives us a sense of meaning.

Studies have also shown that the more we are introduced to new experiences, such as connecting with other people, the more dopamine — that feel-good chemical — the brain produces. We can get these new experiences by connecting with brand new people or connecting at a deeper level with people we already know.

The production of dopamine is not guaranteed with every human connection; it depends on the quality of that interaction, and your interpretation of that connection. If you interpret a human connection as nurturing or empathic, it is likely to produce more dopamine.

So, we don't just need any sort of travel companion in our life. And we certainly do not want one who will lead us away from the well-trodden path and dangerously close to the cliff's edge. We need the right kind of human connection to nurture us, to support us, and to get that all-important dopamine fix. Later in this chapter we will explore what is meant by the "right kind of human connection".

An Affirmative Approach to Relationships with Our Travel Companions

When we refer to a partner, or an intimate relationship, this should be taken as inclusive of all relationship structures, including (but not limited to) polyamory, monogamy, open arrangements, swingers, and consensual non-monogamy.

In addition, when we refer to relationships with our travel companions, this includes personal or working relationships. So, this could be a relationship with a partner (or partners), your friends, or work colleagues.

Relationship Conflict, Anger, and the Male label

When night falls, life's journey becomes so much harder (and sometimes dangerous) if you are alone. Where is that trusted person to watch your back as the Beast of Depression prowls, deterred as long as you keep stoking the campfire? You have to rest at some point, so you need other people to watch your back. Human connection isn't just a nice thing to have, it is a matter of survival.

The Conditioning Associated with the Male Label
As we saw in previous chapters, all of us, no matter our label, are taught certain things about the male label, which include:

- We expect the male labeled to be silent and strong, and so they are expected to remain silent about their vulnerabilities.

- The male labeled are expected to focus outwards, on external gain and power, not inwards, on emotions and thoughts. As a result, even the male labeled themselves may be unaware they experience depression or anxiety.

- The male labeled are expected to remain independent, and so seeking help for something like depression or anxiety is an admission of defeat. As a result, less male labeled are likely to seek help for depression or anxiety, and so the myth continues that the male labeled are somehow untouched by the Beast or the Fireball.

- Due to structural inequality, the problem of a lack of access to mental healthcare by the male labeled is compounded when we consider how the male label intersects with their identity (for example, their racial or ethnic identity, true gender identity, or sexuality).

None of these conditions are ideal for forging deep and meaningful connections with our travel companions. For example, it is hard to sustain a deep and meaningful relationship if one or more parties to that relationship struggle with untreated depression or anxiety, which creates a cycle of

- detachment from emotions;
- withdrawal from travel companions; and
- more anger and irritability.

Mental Workout Routine

Are you aware of this sort of conditioning attached to the male label? Or have you witnessed it in others?

Consider also whether this conditioning has arisen regarding the intersection of the male label and your identity (for example, your racial or ethnic identity, true gender identity, or sexuality). For example, have you experienced structural inequality when attempting to access mental healthcare? Have you experienced any racism, transphobia, biphobia, or homophobia of a healthcare professional? Do you think this has had an impact on any of your relationships?

In the space below, make a note of three examples where you have witnessed this.

1.
2.
3.

The Right Kind of Human Connection

The right kind of connection comprises the following elements:

1.   A healthy balance, free of distortions, and free of abuse in all its forms (physical, emotional, financial, and isolation)
2.   Trust
3.   Secure Attachment
4.   Assertiveness, including assertive communication of all emotions, including anger

We will look at each of these components in turn.

1. A Healthy Balance

As you navigate the wilderness of your life, you need to maintain a healthy, balanced relationship. The last thing you want to do is let one of your travel companions (your partner, colleague, friend, or family member) topple you over the nearest cliff.

Mental Workout Routine

What does a healthy balance look like in a relationship? Use the space set out below to make a note of three components to a healthy, balanced relationship. This is what you think is healthy and balanced, so there is no answer provided.

1.
2.
3.

Compromise

Ever heard the song *Loch Lomond?*

> *"You take the high road, and I'll take the low road, and I'll be in Scotland afore ye..."*

No? The half of me that has Scottish heritage is crying inside. The point is that, contrary to the song's message, we don't have to split up and make life a race to the finish. Could we not take a path that is some place halfway between the high and low roads?
In other words, we could try one of those crucial relationship-cementing C-words:
compromise.

Neither party should silence the other, and even if a decision is made by one person, they need to at least consider the other person's thoughts and emotions. To form a relationship with one of your travel companions, you do not have to surrender your individuality, any more than you should demand this of someone else. This is, after all, a relationship, and not a power grab.

To compromise in a relationship means that you are communicating respect for that other person's thoughts and emotions. It does not mean that you have to agree with what they think or how they feel, but you should at least respect that these are their experiences. Compromise allows space for the thoughts and emotions of your travel companions.

Some refer to this as validation, and when it does not take place, it can lead to a whole avalanche of scary consequences. If you grew up in a household where your caregivers did not understand the concept of compromise, where your thoughts and emotions were constantly invalidated

- You can end up pursuing more unbalanced, unhealthy relationships where there is a glaring lack of compromise, and your thoughts and emotions are invalidated on a daily basis.
- You can end up trying to express those thoughts and emotions through other, less helpful, means, such as
    - excessive work
    - binge eating
    - excessive alcohol
    - drug-taking
    - self-harm
    - suicidal ideation
    - and many more destructive patterns.

As a result, your travel companions are even less likely to strike a compromise with you (not least because you have scared the living daylights out of them with this scary behavior). And so you become invalidated again.

Set Boundaries with Love

Without compromise, without validation of the thoughts and emotions of your travel companions, boundaries become eroded. This can be a subtle process that occurs over time, like coastal erosion of the chalky cliffs of Dover (the Dover in England, not the one in New Jersey), and before you know it, you have no space left to breathe.

Breathing is sort of essential, so let's see how we can set those boundaries. Sometimes I get a bit of pushback from my clients, who claim that boundary setting might come across as rude or obstructive. But you can set boundaries with love (and it is sort of essential if you don't want to run the risk of exploding in a screaming fit, or withdrawing from that travel companion altogether).

<u>Eight Steps to Setting Boundaries (with Love)</u>

<u>Step 1</u> — Use a calm, measured tone.

Boring is better than being bamboozled by battle fatigue.

<u>Step 2</u> — Use *I-statements* such as, "When you cut me off, I feel like you don't care about what I have to say."

This is better than the accusatory, "You cut me off because you want to silence me," especially because you are not a mind reader, and so you do not know, for sure, what they want to do. What you do know is how *you* feel when you are cut off; the *I-statement* is an important part of this. You can only take ownership of your own experiences, not someone else's behavior.

<u>Step 3</u> - Don't be an Ass and Assume.
If there are missing facts (including the intention behind your travel companion's behavior), ask for more

221

information, for example, "Is that what you intended by cutting me off? Did you want me to believe that my views are less important than yours?"

An observation is not an assumption. You can observe and describe someone's shaking fist, and you can say it makes you feel scared, but you cannot assume that the other person intends to hurt or scare you. Observe the person's behavior, describe it, and share how it makes you feel, but let them describe their own intent and feelings behind that observable behavior.

Step 4 - Set the boundary in an open-handed manner. This means that you share how you see things, but you are willing to hear their side, for example, "I would like for you to let me finish when I talk, so I know that you value my views as much as your own. Is this something that seems a reasonable request?"

Step 5 - You may not be heard the first time, so you might need to repeat everything, with the same calm, measured tone. But…

Step 6 - When your travel companion responds, don't just ignore them and repeat like an automaton. Instead…

Step 7 - Confirm you have heard them by offering a quick summary of what they just said.

Step 8 - Show respect for their (perhaps differing) view.

Mental Workout Routine

Think of a time when you felt boundaries should have been set with a travel companion. For example, was a friend using your shore house too often, or did your work colleague take credit for one too many of your projects?

Think of how you responded in that situation, and use the space below to set out the degree to which you followed each of the eight steps to setting boundaries (with love).
When you evaluate your response to this travel companion, make a note of

(1) How much you fulfilled the relevant step. To assess this, award yourself the following points for each step:
0 points = You did not comply with the step at all
1 point = You made a little effort to comply with the step
2 points = You made a reasonable effort to comply with the step
3 points = You fully complied with the step.

(2) If you scored 1 point or less for any step, what could you try next time to fall more in line with this approach to boundary setting?

<u>Eight Steps to Setting Boundaries (with Love)</u>

<u>Step 1</u>

(1) How much you fulfilled the relevant step:

Points awarded for this step (maximum of 3 points):

(2) If you didn't fulfill that step, what could you try next time to get more aligned with this approach to setting boundaries (with love)

Step 2
(1) How much you fulfilled the relevant step:

Points awarded for this step (maximum of 3 points):

(2) If you didn't fulfill that step, what could you try next time to get more aligned with this approach to setting boundaries (with love)

Step 3
(1) How much you fulfilled the relevant step:

Points awarded for this step (maximum of 3 points):

(2) If you didn't fulfill that step, what could you try next time to get more aligned with this approach to setting boundaries (with love)

Step 4

(1) How much you fulfilled the relevant step:

Points awarded for this step (maximum of 3 points):

(2) If you didn't fulfill that step, what could you try next time to get more aligned with this approach to setting boundaries (with love)

Step 5

(1) How much you fulfilled the relevant step:

Points awarded for this step (maximum of 3 points):

(2) If you didn't fulfill that step, what could you try next time to get more aligned with this approach to setting boundaries (with love)

Step 6
(1) How much you fulfilled the relevant step:

Points awarded for this step (maximum of 3 points):

(2) If you didn't fulfill that step, what could you try next time to get more aligned with this approach to setting boundaries (with love)

Step 7
(1) How much you fulfilled the relevant step:

Points awarded for this step (maximum of 3 points):

(2) If you didn't fulfill that step, what could you try next time to get more aligned with this approach to setting boundaries (with love)

Step 8
(1) How much you fulfilled the relevant step:

Points awarded for this step (maximum of 3 points):

(2) If you didn't fulfill that step, what could you try next time to get more aligned with this approach to setting boundaries (with love)

Don't Be Blinded by the Halo Effect

Remember how Beyoncé sang about something that was written all over your face? No? You really don't remember? She saw a "Halo, halo, halo...."

If you look at any of your travel companions, and all you see is a halo shining in your eyes, how are you supposed to make out their actual features? The brightness of the halo will blind you to the defects and bumps that make them less godly, and more human.

Now imagine that you love a certain characteristic of your travel companion. Perhaps they are kind to your parents, or they share the same political views, or they have a similar approach to parenting. This appealing quality might just blind you to other aspects of their personality that are far from appealing. This is known as the "Halo Effect." You like someone, and your overall view of them leads you to blind spots. This can happen in all contexts including -

A Personal Relationship — You are infatuated with someone and overlook their harsh manner towards children.

Business — You trusted that business partner a little too much, because they dazzled you with their intelligence and charm, and you still cannot find the missing funds...

Education — Teachers and lecturers assume students they like are more intelligent than they really are.

Mental Workout Routine

Have you ever met someone you like so much that you overlooked some of their flaws?
Use the space set out below to make a note of
who this travel companion is;
what makes them so appealing; and
what their halo blinds you to.

Identity of travel companion:

Nature of their halo:

What you were blinded to:

The Drama Triangle

The Halo Effect is not the only distortion that can throw a relationship off-balance. Another distortion is the Karpman Drama Triangle. Dr. Stephen Karpman coined this phrase, and it was a development on a theory first introduced by Dr. Eric Berne, a psychiatrist who created an approach to therapy called transactional analysis (TA).

Instead of seeing your travel companions as the rounded human beings that they are, your perception can become distorted by a romantic notion that
    One person is the helpless "victim";
    Making another the evil, *Hooded Claw* "persecutor";
    Leaving the role of knight in shining armor "rescuer" for anyone who wishes to play.

If one person leans in one direction (for example, they adopt the role of victim), that can make others appear to be the persecutor or the rescuer. As a result, people perceive distorted versions of each other in that relationship:

- The victim might view themself as helpless in all situations, thus overlooking any of their strengths and resources
- The victim might overly rely on the rescuer
- The victim's own wrongdoing might be overlooked if their role as a victim is all that is seen
- The rescuer's own vulnerabilities might be overlooked if they are only seen as an almighty rescuer
- The rescuer's own wrongdoing might be overlooked if they are idealized as the rescuer
- The persecutor might become pathologized on the basis of one act or one perception
- The persecutor's own vulnerabilities might be overlooked if they are only seen as a wrongdoer

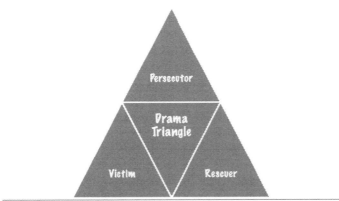

Figure 29 - The Karpman Drama Triangle

If we let our relationships become distorted by the Karpman Drama Triangle, we will never get a healthy, balanced view of our travel companions. You know by now that I do not favor labels as human nature is far more complicated and multifaceted than that and

No person is a wholly helpless victim,

Any more than someone is an evil, *Hooded Claw* persecutor, or

A knight in shining armor rescuer.

We all have good and bad qualities, helpful and unhelpful, and these come out, to varying degrees, depending on the context.

Mental Workout Routine

Looking at the various travel companions in your life, whether your partner, your friends, your family members, or colleagues, are any of your relationships distorted by the Karpman Drama Triangle?

Use the space below to identify one such relationship, and identify who is the victim, the persecutor, and the rescuer.

The relationship

The victim

The persecutor

The rescuer

Freedom from Abuse

The right kind of connection includes a healthy balance, and this includes freedom from abuse in all its forms (physical, emotional, financial, and isolation).

No matter how *Hallmark* movie we try to make life, there are people we need to avoid. Some people use labels (such as toxic, narcissist, sociopath or psychopath) but hurt people hurt people, and I would never pathologize anyone who was acting in an abusive way, However, that does not mean you have to put up with abuse.

<u>When Is It Abuse?</u>

Even if you have known this person forever and a day, even if they have, by chance, been given a certain title in your life (for example, parent, sibling, cousin, best friend, or boss), their behavior might constitute abuse.

Sometimes you only realize it is abuse when it is too late —

after they have called you those names yet again;

when they have shoved you against the wall for the tenth time;

after you discover the lies they have been spreading about you; or

when you look around your life and discover there isn't a corner left that you haven't conceded, that you haven't handed over to them, to make of it what they want.

Then, late at night, with that blind sense of dull panic, you realize the relationship is abusive.

Mental Workout Routine

Do you recognize any of the following signs of abuse?

If you do, use the space set out below to list three examples of abuse you have experienced.

- *They disregard your thoughts and emotions, or they tell you that you "should not" have those thoughts or emotions*
- *They devalue or belittle you*
- *They humiliate you*
- *They harass you with unwanted visits, telephone calls, text messages, or emails*
- *They use demeaning or insulting names when they refer to (or address) you*
- *They show disregard for your suffering (emotional or otherwise)*
- *They show an intent to cause you harm in some way*
- *They threaten or use violence*
- *They try to control you by using any power they have over you. This can include the use of money, status, or sex*
- *They blackmail you (emotionally or otherwise)*
- *They isolate you*

List three examples of your experience of abuse

1.
2.
3.

What to Do about An Abusive Travel Companion?

Once you have become clear that your travel companion's behavior is indeed abusive, you have three options:
1. Pain Management
2. Last Chance Saloon
3. Exit Stage Left

Which option you choose is up to you, and an informed choice would take into account the pros and cons, including short-term versus long-term goals.

Here are some guidelines for making that difficult choice.

1. *"Pain"* management until you can escape

Not everyone can immediately escape an abusive relationship. You might be trapped because of finances, or you fear an immediate bid for freedom might cause more harm (to yourself, or to someone you love). If this is the case, there are ways you can manage the pain of the abuse until you find a way to escape.

The suggestions set out below have helped my clients manage the pain of abuse, as well as the pain of physical illnesses:

- *Enter into the pain:*
  - Based on the mindfulness principles of nonjudgmental acceptance, really tune into the thoughts, emotions, and bodily sensations the abuse evokes in you.
  - Become aware of, and accept, what is, rather than trying to ignore it.
  - Try to be specific when you describe these experiences, but at the same time recognize these thoughts, emotions, and bodily sensations simply as thoughts, emotions, and bodily sensations. If you allow yourself to

experience a distance from these, you might be able to see that they are temporary. And they are not the whole of you.

- *If it feels overwhelming to enter the pain, anchor yourself in the present moment by focusing on each breath:*
  o Allow your thoughts, emotions, and bodily sensations to come and go, but keep returning your attention to each breath.
  o Ask yourself, *"How uncomfortable is it right now?"*
  o No matter the response, refocus on each breath again.
- *Step away from any ideas that you are in some way responsible for the abuse. These statements may help:*
  o "I am not responsible for their actions"
  o "I did not cause their abusive behavior"
  o "They [the abusive travel companion] have failed, but I have not"
  o "They are the sick one"
  o "It is not down to me to change their abusive ways"
  o "I cannot help someone who is unwilling to accept help"
  o "It says jack sh*t about my manhood when I am trying to p*ss on a towering inferno"
- *Create a caricature out of the abusive travel companion:*
  o Imagine your abusive travel companion as a cartoon character with ridiculous features like a beehive hairstyle or huge googly eyes.
  o Add a high-pitched squeal of a voice that gives you a sense of ridicule when you think about their behavior.
  o Do not share this caricature with the abusive travel companion
- *Seek support:*

- o It can be exceptionally hard to manage abusive behavior if you are doing this on your own.
- o Whether it is a trained professional, close friend, or family member, get support so you can stay safe, and get feedback as you work through this.
- *Manage your expectations:*
  - o It is probably unrealistic to hope that this is a one-time solution, and that you will never feel the pain of abuse again.
  - o Manage your expectations by adopting an open-handed approach, quietly acknowledging that if the pain comes again, you have these steps to manage it.
  - o Repeat a calming statement like, "So be it" or "What will be will be."

2. Last Chance Saloon

After carrying out an analysis of the pros and cons, including short-term versus long-term goals, you might decide that the relationship is worth saving at the last chance saloon. This is where you try the three steps set out below.

Step 1 - Acknowledge the abuse, with specific examples
Step 2 - Use assertive communication to
   set boundaries and
   set time limits for a change in their behavior
Step 3 - Review any breach or compliance that took place within those time limits.

3. Exit Stage Left

If there is no hope of change, or you are unwilling to give it more time, or there has been no acceptable change within the time limits you set above, detach with love.

You can choose to detach for a temporary period or permanently. Detaching can be a physical act, but it can also include the emotional; for example, you choose to share less about your life with them.

* * *

2. Trust

So far we have seen that the right kind of human connection includes a healthy balance, free of distortions, and free of abuse in all its forms. Trust is another essential ingredient, and yet because it is so essential, like oxygen or water, we sometimes take it for granted. But when it has disappeared, your relationship is as good as dead.

Give A Little to Get A Little

To sow a healthy crop of trust, you need to give a little. You give to the soil by fertilizing it, and so you give to the relationship, where you hope trust will grow, by giving a few seeds of trust to your travel companion. Give a little trust, and you might see it produce plenty in return.

Trust cannot be seized, and it cannot be demanded. It grows so slowly that you cannot see it flourish, but all of a sudden you notice it is there in all its glory. But it needs the right environment to grow. To ensure optimum growth, you need to create an environment with these three conditions:
> Time and attention
> Forgiveness
> Compassion.

You will recall we discussed one relationship-cementing C-word—*compromise*.

Another is
   compassion.

Mental Workout Routine

We examined the concept of compassion in Chapter 1. Without looking back at that chapter, test your memory by using the space set out below to name three of the five hallmarks of compassion.

The answers are set out below.

1.
2.
3.

Answers

The hallmarks of compassion:
- *kindness*
- *you see suffering and you want it to end*
- *you know that we are all human, and so you recognize that mistakes can be made*
- *you understand rather than criticize or punish*
- *you adopt a mindful, balanced approach to life.*

Only Fools Rush In (and Out)

If you are growing carrots, you don't dump a load of fertilizer on the fragile, early buds of growth. In the same way, when the early buds of a relationship are still forming, you wouldn't throw all your trust at someone and expect them to do the same. That is just a little bit creepy.

Only fools rush in, and out, of trust. At the first signs of growth, you wouldn't yank your crops out of the ground for fear the weather might change and you would lose it all to an early frost. At best you would be left with a few under-developed crops, and that is hardly going to sustain you during life's long journey through the wilderness.

Trust needs time to develop in a way that will sustain and nourish a healthy relationship. Watch carefully, and adjust as appropriate. In the early days, for example, your travel companion might have showed you good reason to trust, but lately they have started to make you doubt their motivations. You might need to pull back a little, until you have understood what is going on. This doesn't mean the whole crop is ruined; it might just have been an off day.

No One-Hit Wonders

One year's healthy harvest of feast might be followed quickly by a drought or flood, leading to a bunch of famished travel companions. In the same way, you don't just open yourself up to trusting a travel companion, and that is it for life, you are ready to trust them one hundred percent, and you will do so forever and a day.

You need to constantly review the trust you have in your travel companions, and there will be times when you need to watch certain travel companions more closely than others. This is especially so if that particular relationship is weathering the storm of economic pressures, stress from parenting, or perhaps one of you is trying to flee from a Fireball of Anxiety, or the Beast of Depression.

This is a message of caution as much as it is a message of hope; don't be a fool who is blind to the facts, even if you have known this person forever. But also, don't assume that the relationship is over because your trust has reduced a little in comparison with the past years. Next year's crop might be more plentiful.

Trust Is About More Than a Label

You can't eat labels, and labels won't help your crops to grow. So, let's ditch them, especially when it comes to trust. How many times do I hear people say, "I am a trusting person," as if they are living in a one-size-fits-all reality. If you are such a "trusting person", try the following:

- Leave your front door open at night*
- Share your bank login details with people, but ask them not to take any money*
- And the next time you drive past someone waiting in the rain at a bus stop, offer to drive them anywhere they like*.
(*Please don't do any of these things.)

Stop with the generalizations. You don't trust everyone, and you don't give all your trust forever to a person. Trust is not a huge label to slap over your eyes so you can take a break from thinking. You need your eyes wide open in life so you can continuously assess each person in each situation, and make a decision about how much trust is appropriate.

The Parasites of Your Low Self-Esteem

There is nothing worse for a crop of trust than for parasites of your low self-esteem to ravage it and destroy any hope of trusting anyone.

Your low self-esteem might have developed as a result of experiences from your past; for example, abusive caregivers when you were young. In such a scenario, it is going to be a great deal harder to trust in your adult life when you fear re-experiencing some of the childhood experiences of being overwhelmed or hurt.

You can learn from the past, but you should not let it hold you hostage. Is the present relationship really the same as the relationship you experienced with your abusive caregivers? We will explore more of this in the next chapter, in which you will find ways to help you distinguish the past trauma from the present reality. In the meantime, have a look at the tips on self-esteem set out in Chapters 1 and 2.

* * *

So far, we have seen that the right kind of human connection includes a healthy balance, free of distortions and abuse, and a healthy crop of trust.

But just look at the journey you still have ahead of you. Life's wilderness is surely going to include some steep mountains that challenge you, and so the safest way to proceed is to ensure that you are securely attached to a travel companion or two. Without this, when you stumble and fall, you will free fall to oblivion.

Remember we mentioned two relationship-cementing C-words, *compromise*, and *compassion*.
A third and final relationship-cementing c-word is
connection — which is all about having a secure attachment to your travel companions.

3. Secure Attachment

The well-established psychological *attachment theory* can help you understand what secure attachment entails, how you generally cope with situations, and what might have gone wrong in a relationship. For example:

241

When your travel companion does not answer a text message, how do you cope?

Does your mind start to race as you keep messaging them until they answer, or

Are you generally the one who ignores the messages?

Attachment Styles

Our earliest childhood experiences (with our caregivers) contribute to our style of attachment to the travel companions in our adult life. Here is what I mean.

<u>Secure Attachment Style</u>
If you had an attentive caregiver who responded diligently to your emotional needs, you might have developed what is called a secure attachment style, the ideal form of attachment that contributes to the right kind of human connection.

When you were an infant, if you felt securely attached to your caregiver, you might have felt they were somehow still protecting you even when they were out of sight.

As a result, now you have grown up and formed adult relationships with your travel companions, you are able to strike a healthy balance of
Intimacy, and
independence.

The hallmark of this secure attachment style is mutual trust. Basically, you trust your travel companions that when you are vulnerable, they will be there for you. You have a healthy form of communication (not too much, but not too little), you can use assertiveness, and you take negative feedback well.

Anxious Attachment Style

If your caregiver failed to respond to your needs, perhaps because they were struggling with their own anxiety or depression, you might have developed an anxious attachment style where you anxiously clung to your caregiver. When they left the room, you did not believe that they would return, and as a child who depends on a caregiver for protection, that can seem devastating.

As a result, as an adult, you form relationships with your travel companions in the following ways:

You crave *intimacy* by becoming clingy, dependent, and preoccupied with the relationship.

You view *independence* as threatening.

Anxious attachment style is characterized by distress when you are separated from your travel companion. For example, you might

- send an excessive number of text messages;
- call frequently when you don't hear back from your travel companion;
- come across as overbearing with a need to spend as much time together as possible;
- tend to overreact, getting stressed out or upset by negative feedback; or
- overshare in the vain hope that this will keep people in your life.

Basically, you constantly question whether your travel companions really care about you. You strike an unhealthy balance of

too much *intimacy*

at the expense of your *independence*.

Avoidant Attachment Style

If your caregiver was unable or unwilling to respond to your needs, you might have developed an avoidant attachment style. The general message you learned is

243

"Why bother?" If your caregiver is not going to respond to your needs, you give up and avoid that attachment. You withdraw in a vain attempt to find the protection you should have gotten from your caregiver.

When you grow up and form adult relationships with your travel companions, you
    avoid *intimacy*; and
    seek out *independence*.

Avoidant attachment is characterized by indifference when you are separated from your travel companions.   For example, you might

- ignore calls or text messages;
- appear aloof or indifferent;
- tend to shut down in the face of negativity; or
- under-share, evoking mistrust and suspicion in others.

As you don't believe that you really need your travel companions you strike an unhealthy balance of
    too little *intimacy*;
    in favor of too much *independence*.

Disorganized Attachment Style
In more severe cases of neglect from caregivers, you might develop a disorganized attachment style, where you cope through a mixture of

- anxious attachment (craving more and more contact, for example); and
- avoidant attachment (pushing or turning away from your caregivers).

You may have received inconsistent messages from your caregiver; at one moment you were loved and protected, and then the next, you were neglected and left to suffer. As a result, you learned to respond in kind, with an equally inconsistent, disorganized approach to people.

In your adult relationships with your travel companions, you oscillate between
> too much and too little *intimacy*; and
> too much and too little *independence*.

With disorganized attachment, there is no consistent pattern in response to your travel companions. You shift erratically from moving towards, and then moving away from, the people around you, leaving your travel companions dazed and confused.

Anxious, Avoidant, and Disorganized Attachment Styles
In all but the secure attachment style, you are likely to hold some or all of these views of yourself, your travel companions, and the world around you:

- *I am not worthy*
- *I am not loveable*
- *My travel companions are not available for true connection*
- *My travel companions are not responsive to my needs*
- *The world is unsafe*
- *The world is unfair*

Mental Workout Routine

If you were to look at your own life, which of the four attachment styles set out above most accurately reflects your own attachment style?

Using the space set out below, note the attachment style, and provide three examples to justify your answer.

Attachment style =
Example #1 =
Example #2 =
Example #3 =

What Can You Do with Your Attachment Style?

The ideal is secure attachment to your travel companions, and because of your early experiences with your caregivers, this might not have been established. If this is the case, consider the following guidance, depending on whether your style is anxious, avoidant, or a mixture of the two (disorganized).

How to Tackle an Anxious Attachment Style

In the case of an anxious attachment style, you crave the intimacy of your travel companions at the expense of the independence of each of you. An anxious attachment style is therefore characterized by a tendency to m*ove towards* your travel companions.

The antidote to the anxious attachment style is to *move away* from your travel companions. This does not mean that you should sell your house and go and live in Antarctica. Instead, you can make subtle adjustments to the balance in your relationships, striving for a more secure attachment style.

To strike a balance between intimacy and independence, consider using some or all of these strategies:

- Text, email, call, visit your travel companions less often.
- Leave longer gaps in between these methods of contact with your travel companions.
- Lessen the intensity of your interactions with those travel companions by sharing less, and expecting less in return.
- Constantly remind yourself that *out of sight does not mean out of mind*. The partners, friends and family members who mean the most will always be there, no matter how infrequent the contact.
- Empathize – How do you imagine your travel companions feel when you basically communicate that you do not trust them unless
  o They answer your fourteenth telephone call within three seconds, or
  o They spend each weekend with you, or
  o They reassure you at every moment?
- Develop a sense of calm composure in the face of negative feedback, and remember that this can be an opportunity to develop a more secure attachment.
- Challenge the assumption that you need to be "perfect" in a relationship.
- Try to establish a healthy sense of self-esteem. Remind yourself of some of the strategies to achieve this by reviewing Chapters 1 and 2.
- "*Role*" with it – Identify travel companions in your life who demonstrate more of a secure attachment style. This role model could be a friend, family member, or even a colleague.
  o How often do they speak to their partner?
  o How many times do they call their own travel companions?

- o And what about text messages, emails, carrier pigeons, and any other forms of communication?
- Meet your own needs – Your attachment style is often an attempt to address your needs, so take a moment to consider what needs you were trying to meet when you sent your travel companion their 20th text message of the day.
  - o Were you feeling insecure in the relationship, and in need of a bit of reassurance?
  - o If so, you don't have to get that reassurance from your travel companion; you could spend a few moments making a list of all the reasons you should feel secure in this relationship.

How to Tackle an Avoidant Attachment Style

In the case of an avoidant attachment style, you crave independence at the expense of intimacy. An avoidant attachment style is therefore characterized by a tendency to *move away* from your travel companion.

The antidote to the avoidant attachment style is to *move towards* your travel companion. This does not mean that you should turn into the stalker who lingers in the bushes outside the home of your favorite travel companion. Yikes.

Instead, make subtle adjustments to the balance in your relationship for a more secure attachment style. Here are some strategies to achieve this balance:

- Text, email, call, visit your travel companions more often.
- Leave shorter gaps in between these methods of contact with your travel companions.

- Increase the intensity of your interactions with those travel companions by sharing more.
- Empathize – How do you imagine your travel companions feel when you basically disappear from their lives every now and again?
- *"Role"* with it – As you saw above, you can identify travel companions in your life who demonstrate more of a secure attachment style. Once you know who they are, find out how often they contact their travel companions, and how long they leave in between each method of contact. And how much do they share?
- Try to establish a healthy sense of self-esteem.
- Meet your own needs – As you saw above, your attachment style is often an attempt to address your needs, so take a moment to consider what needs you were trying to meet by avoiding your best friend for another month:
  - Are you afraid they might hurt you if you let them get too close?
  - If so, spend a few moments making a list of all the positive experiences you have enjoyed with this best friend, and all the evidence that they are someone who you can rely on, and who has not let you down or intentionally hurt you.
  - Also make a list of all the ways that you might be able to cope with any disappointment or hurt if they do make mistakes in the future.

* * *

4. Assertiveness

The right kind of human connection includes assertiveness, which could be described as walking your own path, not treading on toes. I have already exhausted the ass jokes when we looked at assumptions, so I won't repeat those here, but I did find this funny:

"Someone told me to be more assertive, so I am going to try, if that is okay with you."

Assertiveness falls in the middle of these two extremes:

Aggression – An attempt to dominate others without respecting their rights or boundaries.

Passivity – A failure to communicate one's needs, or to allow others to encroach on your boundaries. This could be the result of fear, or an inability to assert one's rights, but it could also be an attempt to manipulate someone.

Sort of like love, you know assertiveness when you see and feel it. I often find that looking at the way we speak can help to identify what is, and what is not, assertiveness.

Aggression – *"I will leave you if you work late tonight."*

Assertiveness – *"I feel lonely when you come home late from work."*

Passivity – *"Fine, work late, see if I care"* (when they really do care).

Mental Workout Routine

How assertive do you think you are? Or, in other words, what is your answer to this question:

How much do you act on other people's wishes at the cost of your own?

Use the space set out below to make a note of your thoughts on this

If you are frequently acting on other people's wishes at the cost of your own, the chances are that you are not very assertive. Similarly, if you are frequently disregarding and railroading other people, you are not very assertive.

If either applies, you need to pay close attention to this section. Assertiveness is an essential component to the right kind of human connection, and it ensures that you live a healthy, balanced life where you survive, but you also thrive. So, one more time for the people in the back: Assertiveness helps you

- thrive in your career;
- develop sustainable business relationships;
- get people to do what you want them to do;
- maintain your personal relationships, so you are not lonely and unfulfilled;
- pursue your personal goals, such as fitness and other interests that can keep your mental well-being nourished and balanced.

So, let's look at what it takes to be assertive.

Assertiveness = Emotional Validity

The most important part of assertiveness is an understanding that your emotions are valid, and so are other people's. You feel a certain way, and no one should tell you otherwise, but you also cannot trample on someone else's toes and tell them what they should or should not feel. Too often I hear people trying to invalidate someone by saying

"You shouldn't feel like that,"
"You are overreacting,"
"You are being melodramatic," or
"No you don't feel that way. "

So, let's be clear: assertiveness is a clear and concise communication of your own emotions, without invalidating your own, or anyone else's, emotions. Emotions are not up for debate.

What you *do* with those emotions is a whole separate question. If you use your sadness to accuse someone of making you sad, that is passivity, not assertiveness. And if you feel frustrated and kick a hole in the wall, that is aggression, not assertiveness. So let's be clear again:

> The actions you take after you have communicated your emotions may or may not be valid. Your actions are up for debate, and they may be right or wrong, depending on the circumstances.
>
> Your emotions are not up for debate.

Assertiveness is the foundation of the right kind of human connection. It is an essential ingredient to a healthy, balanced relationship, and it leads to your own contentment, and the contentment of your travel companions. Assertiveness can help you to get your needs met, meet the needs of others, communicate your feelings, hear the feelings of others, and it can also help to resolve conflict.

How can we get our hands on this magical mystery that is assertiveness?

Six Guidelines for Assertiveness

It may have magical results for your relationships, but there is no mystery about assertiveness.
To be assertive, you simply need to follow these guidelines:

1. Use direct communication.
2. Use a calm, measured tone.
3. Use concise sentences, without apologies.
4. Calmly repeat your points if there is still any confusion or vehement resistance. You can gently acknowledge the other person's perspective, and you can empathize with how they feel, without changing your position. Simply repeat your claim, as if you are a firmly rooted tree swaying in the face of strong winds of opposition.
5. Assertiveness includes the skills of
   1. saying no;
   2. making requests;
   3. giving and receiving criticism. In this respect
   1. be specific;
   2. avoid labels; and
   3. listen to the other person's perspective.
6. You need to decide whether or not to be assertive at any given moment. To help with this decision, you will need to weigh up the cost *versus* the benefit of being assertive. For example, if you really need to keep your job, you might choose not to be assertive to that annoying boss who constantly changes their mind about the project you need to deliver.

Assertiveness Without Being An Asshole

Some people mistranslate
Communicating your emotions is always valid
as
I can be an ass and hurt people.

Too many public figures think they are being honest and "keeping it real" by being rude to people. So let's distinguish assertiveness from *assholeism*.

- *Assholeism* is an attempt to blame another person for your own emotions. It is a fear-driven attempt to manipulate people into agreeing with you, and it happens in all types of personal and working relationships. For example, we have even seen it when a world leader blames marginalized groups for the leader's own prejudices and sense of inadequacy. You are an asshole when you make things about other people, when you are actually talking about your own emotions.

- *Assertiveness* is a communication of your emotions by taking ownership of how you feel. You do not blame anyone for how you feel; it is about you, not them.

<u>Mental Workout Routine</u>

Last week, when Philip was working on a project with a more junior colleague, Raoul, they received some negative feedback from a client. I have set out below three alternative ways Philip reacted to this negative feedback, and I would like you to identify which type of communication applied to which scenario.

The options are
- *aggressive communication;*

- *assertive communication; and*
- *passive communication.*

For 3 bonus points, explain why you have chosen that type of communication. The answers are set out below. And remember: Don't cheat!

Scenario 1 - After the meeting, Philip says nothing about the feedback, and they smile as they go for a drink with Raoul. Afterward, Philip calls Raoul's manager and reports the negative feedback, placing all the blame on Raoul's failings. Philip also neglects to mention anything about Philip's own work on the project.

Type of communication in this scenario:

For 3 bonus points, explain your choice:

Subtotal of bonus points so far: _____

Scenario 2 - After the meeting, Philip shouts at Raoul, accusing them of deliberately neglecting this project in favor of the other two projects. "Something is suspect about all of this," Philip hisses. "Why do you want to sabotage this?"

Type of communication in this scenario:

255

For 3 bonus points, explain your choice:

```

```

Subtotal of bonus points so far: _____

Scenario 3 - After the meeting, Philip tells Raoul, in a calm tone, that Philip feels disappointed. As Philip knows that Raoul has two other projects that have been taking up Raoul's time, Philip asks for the exact amount of hours Raoul has spent on Philip's project.

Type of communication in this scenario:

```

```

For 3 bonus points, explain your choice:

```

```

Subtotal of bonus points so far: _____

Answers:

Scenario 1 — Passive Communication

Why is this Passive Communication? Philip chose not to share their true emotions of disappointment, and they missed the opportunity to find out more information about what happened. Instead, Philip chose to speak to Raoul's boss instead of talking with Raoul about all of this. Without the full facts, Philip made assumptions and, based on these assumptions, Philip damaged their relationship with Raoul.

Even though Raoul is relatively junior now, I have worked with enough people in the corporate world to know that you have to be fair to all people on your way up, because you might pass them on your way down.

Scenario 2 — Aggression

Why is this Aggression? Instead of sharing their emotions in a calm manner, Philip chose to shout. Philip accused Raoul of causing this situation, and this is a much less favorable interaction than trying to negotiate calmly. In addition, Philip tried to read Raoul's mind by claiming Raoul wanted to sabotage Philip's project. Philip knows nothing about what is in Raoul's mind, and a baseless accusation is likely to make Philip look foolish.

Scenario 3 — Assertive Communication

Why is this Assertive Communication? Philip uses a calm tone to communicate their honest emotions. Emotions are always valid, so whether or not Philip should feel disappointed is irrelevant. In addition, Philip takes ownership of their emotions without accusing Raoul of causing them. This is important because Philip and Raoul need a chance to discuss the client feedback; Philip does not yet have all the information, not until Philip has heard Raoul's side of things.

Even if Philip did find out all the relevant information, Philip could improve the situation by making an assertive request that Raoul spend more time on the project, or perhaps get more help. Either way, an accusation is unnecessary.

* * *

The Inconvenience of Anger

Anger is the fart no one wants to admit to. It lingers around, upsetting the overall ambience, and yet we all experience it now and again. And when that *"fart"* comes out in public, or without you meaning it to, it becomes the shameful foghorn of anger that can cause you all sorts of problems.

Foghorns might be fun at a soccer match, but in the quiet confines of your home, or during a tense exchange in a boardroom, it can wreak devastation. Unconstrained anger can risk your career prospects or an important relationship, and it can leave you alone and bitter.

How to Lower the Volume on Your Foghorn of Anger

We have already seen that assertiveness is the foundation of the right kind of human connection to your travel companions, and as assertiveness includes a communication of your emotions, that includes the inconvenient emotion of anger.

Emotions, including anger, are valid, and no one can question whether you should or should not feel that way.

What you *do* with that anger is up for debate. For example, you might choose to tell someone, calmly, that you are feeling angry, and it is rare that this would be considered wrong. But if you kick the cat, the wall, the glass window, or anything but a soccer ball, this connected action will, of course, be judged.

Mental Workout Routine

Think of a time when you were last angry.

Use the space below to make a note of what was happening, including what made you angry.

```

```

Thinking of that last time you were angry, use the six guidelines for assertiveness set out earlier in this chapter to score (on a scale of 0 to 5) how much you complied with each guideline where

  0 = you failed miserably, and
  5 = you did exactly what the guideline suggested.

If the guideline did not apply in the circumstances, you automatically score 5 points. For example, if there was an impossible power imbalance (because you were working with a tyrant of a boss), then reward yourself the full 5 points for that guideline.

  1. Did you use direct communication? Score yourself on a scale of 0 to 5, and make a note of the words you used

```

```

  2. Did you use a calm, measured tone? Score yourself on a scale of 0 to 5

```

```

3.   Did you use concise sentences, without apologies? Score yourself on a scale of 0 to 5

4.   If you met resistance, did you calmly repeat your points? Score yourself on a scale of 0 to 5

5.   Did you make use of any of the following assertiveness skills?

Saying no – Score yourself on a scale of 0 to 5

Making requests – Score yourself on a scale of 0 to 5

Giving and receiving criticism. If you gave or received criticism, did you:

Remain specific? Score yourself on a scale of 0 to 5

Avoid labels? Score yourself on a scale of 0 to 5

Listen to the other person's perspective? Score yourself on a scale of 0 to 5

6.   *Weighing it all up, did the benefit of being assertive outweigh any costs? Score yourself on a scale of 0 to 5:*

Total score (out of 50) _____

If you scored between 0 and 25, you could work on your assertiveness when it comes to anger, so carry out a quick review of the assertiveness section set out earlier in this chapter.

If you scored between 26 and 50, well done, and award yourself 3 bonus points. You have mastered the skill of assertiveness (at least for anger), so move onto the next section.

Subtotal of bonus points so far: _____

How to Break the Anger Cycle

To get beyond the blue of your anger, you need to break a cycle similar to the cycles of depression and anxiety:

Your Action Pack (behavior) – You lash out, you drive faster, you cut ahead of others in line, and then your thoughts become more fast and furious.

Your Head Gear (thoughts) – The faultier your Head Gear, the quicker your temper. Whether it is short-circuited by a dodgy filter, overgeneralizations, labeling, or any of the other faults, when you use faulty Head Gear you end up viewing the world as a war zone.

Your Flashlight (emotions) – Like any battle-worn veteran, eventually the Flashlight starts to drain, and as your emotions dim, you want to do less of the things that once brought you joy.

And so the anger cycle continues.

Figure 30 - The Anger Cycle

But it does not have to be this way. As we saw in the previous chapters, the more familiar you are with your Survival Tools, the easier it will be to use them to break free of the anger cycle.

* * *

Survival Tool #1 – Action Pack (Behavior)

Old, New, and Borrowed, to Get you Beyond the Blue

You can break the anger cycle by engaging in actions that once made you feel calm (the old), or you can create new experiences from your own brainstorming (the new), or from ideas that are borrowed from others (the borrowed).

When you gather this list of actions, try to be aware also of the actions or people that increased the likelihood of the occurrence, frequency, or intensity of your anger. You will want to make sure you keep these on a "Banned Actions" list and a "Banned People" list.

Mental Workout Routine

Use the space set out below to answer these questions to identify the components to your Action Pack. Try to gather as many examples as possible, so your Action Pack is varied and plentiful.

What has made you feel calm and contented in the past? What is likely to again? What ideas do you have from other people to create this calm and contented state?

Were there any particular people in your life who made you feel safe and secure, or peaceful and relaxed? Who is likely to again? What ideas do you have from other people to create this safe, secure, peaceful, and relaxed state?

What activities should be on your "Banned Actions" (activities to avoid) list? These are activities likely to increase the occurrence, frequency, or intensity of your anger.

What people should be on your "Banned People" (people to avoid) list? These are people likely to increase the occurrence, frequency, or intensity of your anger.

Lighten the Load of Your Action Pack

As you saw in previous chapters, you do not want to overload your backpack with activities in which you will never engage. That will only increase your anger. Shortlist the above selection by making sure they pass at least one of these tests:

1. *The Test of Mastery* – Do the actions on your list help you develop a sense of mastery?

2. *The Test of Opposite Attraction* – Try to ensure that the actions on your list evoke the opposite of anger.

3. *The Test of Appreciation* – Do the actions on your list make you appreciate what you have?

Mental Workout Routine

Create a short list of the components to your Action Pack that passed the Test of Mastery, the Test of Opposite Attraction, or the Test of Appreciation

A SMART Action Pack

As we saw earlier in this Survival Guide, you need to use the SMART approach to plan how and when you are going to engage in the actions you have packed. Look at the earlier chapters to remind yourself of how to make a SMART Action Pack.

Mental Workout Routine

Choose at least three components to your Action Pack and use the blank grid (Figure 31) below to assess whether each item is SMART.

If it is not SMART, what do you need to change to make it a SMART Action?
Don't forget to also use the blank schedule below (Figure 32) to make each component to your Action Pack Time-bound.

Item from your Action Pack	Specific?	Measur-able?	Achiev-able?	Realistic?	Time-bound? Use the Action Planner below to create a schedule for each SMART Action compone nt.

Figure 31 - How to Make Your Action Pack SMART

To make each component to your Action Pack Time-bound -

Component to your Action Pack	Time	Day, and frequency	Intensity
1			
2			
3			

Figure 32 - How to Make Your Action Pack Time-bound

*   *   *

As we saw earlier in this Survival Guide, your Action Pack is the quickest and easiest of the three Survival Tools to use. But it alone does not always help you to break free of the anger cycle.

* * *

Survival Tool #2 – Head Gear (Thoughts)

You have seen how your Action Pack (your behavior) can keep you trapped in the anger cycle as much as it can break you free. The same can be said for your Head Gear (your thought process).

As Simple as A-B-C

As we've seen earlier in this Survival Guide, the ABC log is a tool used to help understand how your Head Gear can help and hinder you.

If you need a reminder of the basics about the ABC log, have a look at earlier chapters in this Survival Guide.

Mental Workout Routine

Use the blank ABC log that is set out below (see Figure 33) to record an example of when you last felt angry. Complete columns A, B, and C for now.

A	B	C	D	E
Activating Event	Beliefs & Assump-tions	Conse-quences	Dispute	Evaluate

Figure 33 - ABC Log

Column A – The Activating Event (Trigger)

The activating event (or trigger) refers to what was happening at the time of your anger:
- What was going on?
- Who was involved?
- Was there anything out of the ordinary about what you were doing, or what others were doing around you?

Column B – Beliefs and Assumptions

At the time of the activating event, what were your beliefs or assumptions? For example, were you carrying around an unhelpful belief such as "*I am unsafe*"?

Which of the seven common faults were impeding your Head Gear?

1. All-or-nothing thinking

2. Emotional reasoning
3. Putting the ass in assumptions
4. The tyranny of the shoulds
5. Personalization
6. Catastrophic thinking
7. Dodgy filter, overgeneralizations, and labeling

If you need a reminder of the detail of these faults, have a look at the earlier chapters in this Survival Guide.

Column C – Consequences (Emotional and Behavioral)

As a result of the activating event you noted in column A, and the beliefs and assumptions you noted in column B:

- How do you feel? How would you rate your anger on a scale of 0 to 10, where
  - 0 = not angry at all, and
  - 10 = intensely angry.

- What did you do?

Column D – Disputing or Correcting Beliefs and Assumptions

To break the anger cycle, you need to fix any faults in your Head Gear.

Here is a quick reminder of how to fix each of the seven common faults. For the detail on each, have a look at the earlier chapters in this Survival Guide.

1. All-or-Nothing Thinking
Think in terms of shades of grey, and find a middle ground.

2. Emotional Reasoning
Balance your emotions with other sources of information, including logic, an analysis of all the facts, and proportionality.

3. Putting the Ass in Assumptions
To stop making assumptions, check that you have all the facts, and stop trying to mind read.

4. The Tyranny of the Shoulds
Try replacing your shoulds and musts with a preference, "I would like," or "I prefer."

5. Personalization
Who or what else is involved?

6. Catastrophic Thinking
Scale down your language, as few things are *catastrophic, urgent,* or even *imperative.*

7. Dodgy Filter, Overgeneralizations, and Labeling
Adopt a balanced approach by incorporating the good and bad in an evaluation, and resist the overgeneralization of a label. Be specific.

Mental Workout Routine

Turn again to the blank ABC log (see Figure 33). Previously, you filled out columns A, B, and C for when you were last angry.

Now have a go at filling out column D; try to fix any faults in your Head Gear you have identified in column B.

271

Column E Is for Evaluating

Mental Workout Routine

Turn again to the blank ABC log (see Figure 33). Previously, you filled out columns A, B, C, and D for when you were last angry.

Now have a go at filling out column E by:

Re-evaluating your Beliefs
Re-evaluate any beliefs and assumptions (as identified in column B) on a scale where
> *1 = you don't really believe it, and*
> *7 = you wholeheartedly believe it.*

Create a new, more constructive belief to replace the above-mentioned beliefs if you found them unhelpful. For example, instead of the absolute, "I am unsafe", you could replace it with a more helpful, "I have ways of keeping myself safe".
   Try to give this new belief a rating from 1 to 7, where
> *1 = you don't really believe it, and*
> *7 = you wholeheartedly believe it.*

Re-evaluate your Emotions
Re-evaluate your anger (as identified in column C) on a scale of 0 to 10, where
> *0 = no anger, and*
> *10 = intense anger*

The theory is that you may, eventually, see a decrease in this level of distress.

Continue to monitor yourself and reflect on how you are progressing with this.

* * *

Survival Tool #3 – Your Flashlight (Emotions)

Remember how you used your Flashlight to break free of the depression cycle, and the anxiety cycle? In the same way, you can use this Survival Tool to break free of the anger cycle.

Have a look at the earlier chapters of this Survival Guide if you need a quick reminder of the importance of this Survival Tool.

Component 1
The Multicolored Words of the Flashlight

Instead of just anger, perhaps you are feeling lonely, sad, or hopeless. So you are not left feeling even more frustrated, you need the full palette of emotions to clearly, and more accurately, communicate your needs.

Remember also to name the intensity of the emotion. You can use a scale of 0 to 10, where
> 0 = A very low level of intensity
> 10 = An intense level of intensity

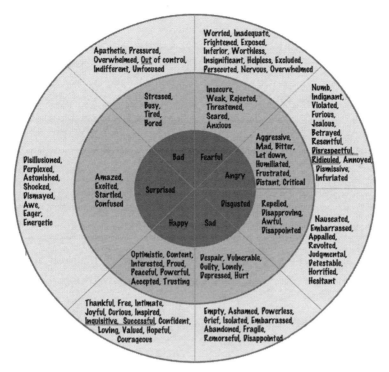

Figure 34 - The Full Spectrum of Your Emotions

Component 2
The Power Pack in your Flashlight

The intensity of your anger will be significantly impacted by the following sources of power for your Flashlight:

- Sleep, food, drink
- Drugs, prescription or otherwise
- Exercise
- The absence of stressful experiences over a recent period
- The extent to which you have over/under-scheduled yourself.

Mental Workout Routine

Use the grid set out below (Figure 35) to identify your own patterns in the intensity of your anger.

Day	Sleep Schedule	Consumption of food, drink, and drugs	Exercise	Stressful experiences?	Over/Under-scheduled?
Monday					
Tuesday					
Wednesday					
Thursday					
Friday					
Saturday					
Sunday					

Figure 35 - How to Master the Intensity of Your Flashlight

Component 3
Master the Dimmer Switch

To regulate your anger and master the Dimmer Switch, you can use any of the following techniques:

Stimulate Your Five Senses to ground yourself (this is the grounding exercise detailed in Chapter 2).

Engage Your Breathing Apparatus so you can activate your ventral vagal nerve network, reducing the harmful cortisol (stress hormone) (this is the breathing exercise detailed in Chapter 2).

Activate The Power Pack of your Imagination to visualize a calmer scene (this is the visualization exercise detailed in Chapter 2).

These give you space to choose how to respond to your triggers, so you can cope with your anger in a healthier, less reactive way. If you need a reminder of each step of these exercises, review Chapter 2.

Surf the Light Waves of Each Emotion

As you saw in earlier parts of this Survival Guide, you can learn how to manage emotions by remembering that each emotion, including anger, is like a light wave, and has
A beginning (or a buildup),
A middle (a peak), and
An end (it subsides).

You can see this in Figure 36.

Figure 36 - How to Surf the Light Waves of Your Emotions

If you use a mindful approach to observe your anger without trying to change it, if you stay with the anger (the emotion, not acting on it) during the buildup and peak, you will eventually experience the anger subside. When you do this, you learn you have resilience, and you do not need to keep acting on the anger by lashing out (at others, or yourself).

* * *

Shelter of Resilience

Sometimes the foghorn of anger can blast so loudly that you need the peace of silence that can be found within the Four Walls of your Shelter of Resilience. If you need a reminder of how to construct and maintain this Shelter, have a look at Chapter 1.

* * *

If You Are in Crisis

If you find yourself beyond the blue of your relationship conflict, and anger has got you to the point of crisis, seek immediate, professional help. Please turn to Appendix Crisis for further information.

* * *

Survive and Thrive Recap

In this chapter, you

- learned about the benefit of human connection;
- explored the conditioning surrounding relationship conflict, anger, and the male label, including
  - the intersection of the male label with your racial or ethnic identity, true gender identity, or sexuality;
- identified the elements of the right kind of human connection, including

- o a healthy balance, free of distortions, and free of abuse in all its forms (physical, emotional, financial, and isolation),
  - o trust,
  - o secure attachment, and
  - o assertiveness, including assertive communication of all emotions, including anger,
- learned how to use your three Survival Tools to break free of the anger cycle
- were also reminded about the importance of the Four Walls of your Shelter of Resilience.

We need to let our imagination go beyond the blue of the male label. If we can accept that relationship conflict and anger can be symptoms of untreated depression and anxiety, and this lack of treatment is (in part) due to misconceptions about the male label, and, in some cases, due to structural obstacles, we can give help to those who need it. This will lead to a safer and healthier society for all, before we are lost beyond the blue of relationship conflict and anger.

But relationship conflict and anger are not just symptoms of untreated depression and anxiety. Untreated trauma can also have a significant impact on relationship conflict and anger, but for this we need a slightly different approach.

This is what we turn to next in our journey together.

CHAPTER 5

BEYOND THE BLUE OF YOUR TRAUMA

In the dead of night, you hear the cry of a hawk, and your body freezes with fear. Your eyes are wide, your blood is pumping, and your heart is in your throat. Without a moment to think, you are in *fight-or-flight* mode, a primal instinctual response to an imaginary attack.

You curse yourself for overreacting. *It was just a hawk,* you tell yourself, but you are not responding to the cool light of present-day logic. Your brain is unable to perform to its optimum level because it is crushed under the weight of a *Ten-Ton Trauma*. The past is present.

Trauma — Close Encounters of the Violent Kind

Trauma usually involves experiences that overwhelm, shock, or terrify you. It is often associated with powerlessness and shame, and it goes beyond the much talked about incidents of car crashes and war zones. You can experience trauma as a result of the accumulation of adverse experiences during childhood or adulthood, and at the hands of your caregivers, partner, or a complete stranger. Whether you are the survivor of the terrifying experience, or you witness it happening to someone else, you can still end up with these same hopeless messages:

- *I am powerless*
- *Life is hopeless*
- *No one cares*
- *The world is unsafe*
- *No one can be trusted*

- *I feel disconnected from myself, others, and the world around me*
- *I am broken.*

Trauma can result in a belief that it is no longer possible to
- have control;
- have connection; and
- have meaning.

The Multiple Dimensions of the Ten-Ton Trauma

Do you recognize any of these signs of the Ten-Ton Trauma?

Hyperarousal
- You constantly expect danger.
- You are on edge, jumpy, nervous, angry and irritable, making it hard to sleep or concentrate on work, school, and your home life.
- You see red, and lash out (verbally or physically), at yourself or others.

Intrusion
- You relive moments from the trauma in the form of flashbacks or associated images, sounds, smells, and overwhelming emotions.
- You are disturbed by incessantly negative thoughts about yourself, others, and the world around you.

Hypoarousal
- You feel numb, blank, or vacant.
- You feel detached from yourself, others, or the world around you.
- You zone out so that you do not notice your surroundings, and time slips by.
- Another word people use is "dissociation" — this is a survival mechanism to cope with overwhelming

distress. Think of the saber-toothed tiger that is just about to bite; the last thing you want is to feel the teeth go in, so your mind checks you out of your body. When you experience trauma, you can get stuck in this dissociative state, and you tend to check in and out of our body, even when the threat has long since passed.

Mental Workout Routine

Reading about trauma can be heavy going, so I am going to intersperse throughout this chapter some moments to take a break.

Here's the first: For five or ten minutes, allow yourself to take a breather in any way you need to. This could be one of the following suggestions, or something you choose:
- *Go for a walk around the block*
- *Engage in some light exercise*
- *Talk to a friend*
- *Watch something that makes you smile or laugh*
- *Meditate*
- *Do some stretching, whether it is some formal yoga or Pilates, or informal wriggling your limbs around*

Dizzying Dialectics

Crushed under the weight of ten tons of trauma, you feel dizzy when you try to fathom out a combination of contradictory experiences:

You feel too little — One moment you are numbed to life. You feel vacant in body and mind, as if the world were a strange and unfamiliar place you view through a fog,

You feel too much — Another moment you are the opposite of numb; you feel everything, every moment, so much so that you become overwhelmed by it all. You are flooded with emotions, memories, or images.

Mental Workout Routine

Take a moment to reflect on the descriptions of trauma as set out above.
Do any of the descriptions of trauma resonate with you?
If so, make a note of that description, and when you first noticed this.
What was going on in your life at that time?
Do you have any preliminary ideas about what might have made you feel this way?

The description of trauma that resonated with me, and when I first noticed this.

What was going on in my life when I started to notice this.

Preliminary ideas about what might have started to make me feel this way.

The Toxic Trio of Trauma

Every person's experience of trauma is unique, but there does tend to be a familiar pattern that forms a toxic trio of

1. a sense of terror;
2. a sense of being overwhelmed; and
3. an intense shame.

1.   Terror

The Ten-Ton Trauma can leave you in a state of wide-eyed terror. Frozen and numb, the frontal lobes of your brain shut down, particularly a part called Broca's area, and this means language cannot be processed. Trauma can literally leave you speechless and unable to fully process your experience. The only thing you can comprehend is the intense panic, anger, and helplessness the terror evokes.

2.   Overwhelm

Crushed under the weight of a Ten-Ton Trauma, you have no sense of control over your life. You are overwhelmed, and this can often lead to helplessness. What you once knew to be safe and known becomes an unsafe world of uncertainty.

3.   Shame

As a result of the powerlessness you experienced when you were overwhelmed, you are sickened by a sense of shame. You ruminate over how things could have been different if you had not experienced this trauma, and what you could have done differently to produce a different outcome.

* * *

Help Beyond the Labels

Trying to draw a clear line between "trauma" and "no trauma" is like drawing a line between one emotion and the next. As a result, we need to exercise caution when it comes to diagnostic labels and trauma. For example, a professional might adopt such a narrow interpretation of a person's behavior, thoughts, and emotions that they fail to identify the trauma, leaving that person crushed under the ten-ton weight. As we will see, this risk increases if you are male labeled, and this risk also increases when the male label intersects with your identity.

Nevertheless, some people find the certainty of labels comforting, and so, for completeness here are some of the diagnostic labels that are associated with trauma.

Post-Traumatic Stress Disorder (PTSD)

If you experience, witness, or indirectly experience an event that threatened death or harm to yourself or others, you might end up with a diagnosis of post-traumatic stress disorder (PTSD).

To qualify for this diagnosis, you must also experience some of the following symptoms for more than 30 days. In some cases, these symptoms can be experienced for years.

Intrusive thoughts— These are repeated, involuntary memories, distressing dreams, or flashbacks of the traumatic event.

Sense of threat — As a result of an ongoing sense of threat, you might feel constantly on edge, jumpy, irritable, and restless. You might have angry outbursts, and behave recklessly, and you might have problems concentrating or sleeping.

Avoidance — You might avoid reminders of the traumatic event by avoiding certain people or places, or you might not have memories of certain times.

Re-experiencing — You relive moments from the trauma in the form of flashbacks or associated images, sounds, smells, and overwhelming emotions.

Negative thoughts and emotions — You might hold distorted beliefs about yourself, others, or the world around you such as *I am not safe, I am defective, No one can be trusted, or The world is a cruel place.* You might also experience ongoing emotions of fear, shame, terror, and anger.

<u>Complex Post-Traumatic Stress Disorder (C-PTSD)</u>

If you experienced multiple traumas, particularly when you were growing up, this can lead to complex post-traumatic stress disorder (C-PTSD). The usual case for C-PTSD is where you have, as a child, suffered abuse at the hands of your caregivers.

The "C" of C-PTSD suggests the complexity of the power dynamic between you and your caregivers; as a child, you were trapped because you depended on your caregivers for food and shelter. You might have had to bend yourself out of shape to endure this trauma, because you were faced with an impossible choice: endure the abuse or fail to survive.

In addition to the symptoms of PTSD that are set out above, you might also experience

- interpersonal disturbances (for example, a significant inability to form relationships with people);
- a pervasively negative self-image; and
- an extremely off-kilter ability to regulate your emotions. For example, you might get extremely and intensely sad or angry very quickly, and without an ability to bring things back into a state of equilibrium.

Acute Stress Disorder

This feels similar to PTSD, but it lasts for less time (no more than 30 days).

There are other diagnoses related to trauma, including dissociative identity disorder, but this is beyond the scope of this Survival Guide.

When the Ten-Ton Trauma descends, crushing you with its weight, the label is less important than the help you need to get; suggestions follow later in this chapter, and also in Chapter 6.

* * *

The Trauma of Adverse Childhood Experiences

As you saw from the previous section, trauma is not just a sudden, single incident of violence in the form of a road accident or war zone. Trauma includes an accumulation of negative experiences where there is an imbalance of power, and you have no means of escape. In particular, trauma includes Adverse Childhood Experiences (ACEs) such as:

1.   Growing up in a household where adults swore at you, humiliated you, or made you afraid that you might be physically hurt.

2.　　　Growing up in a household where adults physically hurt you.

3.　　　You experienced sexual abuse.

4.　　　You grew up believing that your family did not think you were special.

5.　　　Your physical needs were not met (for example, food and clothing).

6.　　　Your parents divorced or separated.

7.　　　You witnessed domestic violence.

8.　　　Someone in your household had a problem with drink or drugs.

9.　　　Someone in your household struggled with mental health issues.

10.　　Someone in your household went to prison.

Mental Workout Routine

Did you experience any Adverse Childhood Experiences (ACEs) during the first eighteen years of your life? Check each of the ten criteria below, and give yourself 1 point for each.

1. *Growing up in a household where adults swore at you, humiliated you, or made you fear you might be physically hurt.*
   Score = 0 or 1 _____

2. *Growing up in a household where adults physically hurt you.*
   Score = 0 or 1 _____

3. *You experienced sexual abuse.*
   Score = 0 or 1 _____

4. *You grew up believing that your family did not think you were special.*
   Score = 0 or 1 _____

287

5. *Your physical needs were not met (for example, food and clothing).*
   Score = 0 or 1 _____

6. *Your parents divorced or separated.*
   Score = 0 or 1 _____

7. *You witnessed domestic violence.*
   Score = 0 or 1 _____

8. *Someone in your household had a problem with drink or drugs.*
   Score = 0 or 1 _____

9. *Someone in your household struggled with mental health issues.*
   Score = 0 or 1 _____

10. *Someone in your household went to prison.*
    Score = 0 or 1 _____

If your score on the above Mental Workout Routine added up to 4 or more, your health is likely to be impacted in the following ways:

- Neurobiologists claim that Adverse Childhood Experiences (ACEs) can cause us to get stuck in the fight-or-flight response, which can produce toxic stress, an overproduction of stress hormones such as cortisol and adrenaline.

- The overproduction of stress hormones can harm the structure and function of the brain, and this is particularly significant when we are young, when our brains are still taking shape. After all, the prefrontal cortex (how we can think rationally, logically, and calmly) only fully develops by age 25.

• Studies show that the toxic stress your body endured during these Adverse Childhood Experiences (ACEs) is likely to cause arthritis, heart disease, diabetes, and lung cancer. If you live in a constant fight-or-flight state, adrenaline and cortisol continue to be pumped around your body, your blood pressure remains high, your heart weakens, and your body keeps glucose and cholesterol levels too high. In the end, your body is literally exhausted and depleted.

• Some studies show that toxic stress can also change how your DNA functions, and this can be passed on to the next generation. This is a fascinating area of psychology called epigenetics.

However, all is not lost.

Researchers have found that, because of neuroplasticity, your brain can literally heal itself from trauma. You create new neural pathways as you teach yourself that
- life is not always unsafe;
- some people can be trusted; and
- you are not always to blame.

Example

Charles's Ten-Ton Trauma

Charles's parent was bored and discontent because they did not work, and so they regularly took their frustrations out on Charles. Even from five or six years old, Charles was regularly beaten with a belt, a wooden spoon, the remote control, or anything else the parent could find. The parent made a point of becoming

289

friends with other parents and teachers, and so either people did not suspect the abuse, or they turned a blind eye to the purple-tinted skin and the occasional flinch from Charles.

If anyone had asked Charles, they would have told them that it was not the muffled moment of impact that hurt the most, but the sound of their parent running up the stairs in pursuit of Charles. This would make Charles's blood run cold.

As a result of this ongoing trauma, Charles's Survival Tools were impacted in the following ways:

Charles's Action Pack (Behavior)
As an adult, Charles tended to avoid close relationships altogether. This was partly because Charles felt unsafe in the world. Charles also did not believe in their own worth or ability, and acted in a way that communicated this to others. This became a self-fulfilling prophecy because if someone does not appear to believe in themselves, others are unlikely to.

Charles's Head Gear (Thoughts, Beliefs, and Assumptions)
Charles developed the belief *I am not safe* in the world. Charles also developed the belief *I am inadequate*, because their parent often claimed Charles deserved the beatings for being "annoying," "untidy," and "insolent." Charles carried these beliefs into adulthood, long after the beatings stopped.

Charles's Flashlight (Emotions) and Dimmer Switch)
As a child, Charles would often pass a point of overwhelm during the beatings, and ceased feeling the pain of their parent's fist at all. Charles's mind had checked out, leaving their body to take the beatings. This survival technique, known as dissociation, is something Charles still notices, even in adulthood. This

can cause problems when people think that Charles is being "rude" when they appear not to be listening, and previous partners have accused Charles of being "emotionally distant."

Ever Flipped Your Lid?

To help you understand why the Ten-Ton Trauma can cause such devastation in your life, we need a quick navigation of different parts of your brain.

> The Brain Stem — This helps you to breathe, regulates your balance, keeps your circulation in check, and it is responsible for arousal. This is represented by the palm of the hand, as shown in the images below.
>
> The Limbic System — This processes your emotions and memories. This is represented by the thumb in the images below.
>
> The Prefrontal Cortex — This helps your cognitive process, helping you to think and remain mindful of experiences. This is represented by the fingers in the images below.

All Calm on the Lid Front

Usually, when you are calm and you feel safe, your limbic system is neatly tucked away under your prefrontal cortex.

You can see in (Figure 37) that the thumb (resembling our limbic system) is neatly tucked under your fingers (and remember, the fingers resemble your prefrontal cortex — how you think rationally).

Figure 37- All Calm on the Lid Front

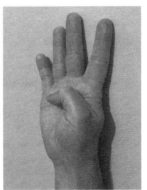

Figure 38 - When You Have Flipped Your Lid

Danger!

When you perceive a threat (imagined or real), your brain "flips the lid" (these are the words of Dr. Dan Siegel, Clinical Professor of Psychiatry at UCLA School of Medicine). This means that your limbic system becomes aroused, and the fight-or-flight response is activated. You can see from (Figure 38) that the fingers of the prefrontal cortex are now raised.

As your prefrontal cortex helps you to think and remain mindful, cool hard logic goes out the window and you become startled and scared. You are no longer a rational intellectual who muses on the meaning of life; you have become primal in your fight-or-flight response, and this is far from useful if there is no actual danger. You have only imagined the threat in the form of the sudden bang of a door, or the smell of cologne that reminds you of a past trauma.
Past becomes present.

If you are to live a peaceful and successful life, you need to stop flipping your lid at every moment.

Mental Workout Routine

Have you ever flipped your lid? Use the space set out below to make a note of what happened, who was involved, and how you handled this.

When you flipped your lid

```

```

Who was involved

```

```

How you handled this

```

```

Charles's Ten-Ton Trauma and Lid Flipping

Remember Charles and their abusive parent? Even decades after the beatings, Charles would still get panicked by the sound of running on stairs (triggering memories of their parent running after Charles with the parent's weapon of choice).

Despite the passage of time, Charles's brain was still flipping its lid. The sound of footsteps on the stairs would arouse Charles's limbic system, activating the fight-or-flight response, leaving Charles without the use of their prefrontal cortex, and thus unable to distinguish past from present.

* * *

Ten-Ton Trauma and the Male Label

In patriarchal societies such as the United States, the male sex label is associated with assumed power and privilege. Focusing on one type of trauma, sexual violence —

there is a significantly higher rate of female-labeled survivors of sexual violence; and
there is a significantly higher rate of male-labeled perpetrators of sexual violence.

However, to *only* take a binary approach to statistics relating to sexual violence is to overly simplify the picture. I have already established that people cannot be easily categorized according to these binary sex labels. The statistics relating to sexual violence is a great deal more complicated when we consider how the sex label intersects with a person's identity (for example, racial and ethnic identity, true gender identity, and sexuality). For example, there are higher numbers of survivors of sexual violence amongst people who are transgender.

In addition, if we are to acknowledge these statistics, we also need to acknowledge:

- There are male-labeled survivors of all types of trauma, including sexual violence.
- It is estimated that 61% of the male labeled in the United States report exposure to at least one traumatic event (SAMHSA).
- That number is much higher when we consider the intersection of the male label with a person's identity (racial or ethnic identity, true gender identity, or sexuality). We will cover more of this later in this chapter when we explore the trauma of marginalized stress and microaggressions (resulting from societal privilege).

Any person's untreated trauma has the potential to harm the whole of society, and the male labeled are less likely to seek (or get) adequate help for trauma. As discussed, this has a great deal to do with the conditioning associated with the male label.

- We expect the male labeled to be silent and strong, and so they are expected to remain silent about their vulnerabilities, including the toxic trio of trauma: terror, overwhelm, and shame.
- The male labeled are expected to focus outwards, on external gain and power, not inwards, on emotions and thoughts. As a result, even the male labeled themselves may be unaware that what they experience is trauma.
- The male labeled should remain independent, so seeking help is an admission of defeat, and this only serves to exacerbate the shame that they

may already experience as a result of their trauma. As a result, if less of the male labeled seek help for trauma, this serves to perpetuate the myth that the male labeled are somehow untouched by the Ten-Ton Trauma.

- Due to structural inequality, the problem of a lack of access to mental healthcare by the male labeled is compounded when we consider how the male label intersects with their identity (for example, their racial or ethnic identity, true gender identity, or sexuality).

As mentioned earlier, trauma can leave you in a bewildering state of

Hyperarousal, where you feel constantly on edge, jumpy, nervous, angry and irritable. If a healthcare professional has preconceived notions about the male labeled, they may end up dismissing your behavior as anger or aggression, rather than untreated trauma;

Intrusion, where you relive moments from the trauma in the form of flashbacks. Again, all that may be interpreted as erratic and disorderly behavior that is pathologized as "problematic," rather than symptoms of an underlying trauma;

Constriction, where you feel numb, blank, or vacant. We have seen in earlier chapters that some healthcare professionals have misguided beliefs that the male labeled are inherently unable to experience emotions, or that they are inherently violent and aggressive. Again, this may mean that the trauma is never discovered and treated.

As you saw in previous chapters, the male labeled are more likely to be diagnosed with an externalizing disorder such as attention-deficit disorder, oppositional defiant disorder, conduct disorder, antisocial personality disorder, or substance-related disorders. This may be in part due to a missed opportunity to identify any underlying trauma. If you add to this the racism, transphobia, biphobia, or homophobia of the diagnosing healthcare professional, the risk of undetected trauma only increases.

Mental Workout Routine

Have you had any experience of this sort of conditioning related to the male label?
If so, do you think this has had an impact on your experiences of trauma?
If you have not experienced trauma, do you know someone who has?
What were their experiences, and do you think this conditioning impacted their experiences of trauma?

Consider also whether this conditioning has arisen regarding the intersection of the male label and your identity (for example, your racial or ethnic identity, true gender identity, or sexuality). For example, have you experienced structural inequality when attempting to access mental healthcare? Have you experienced any racism, transphobia, biphobia, or homophobia of a healthcare professional?
Do you think this has had an impact on your trauma (or the trauma you have witnessed in others)?

In the space below, make a note of three thoughts relating to all of this.

1.

2.

3.

*   *   *

The Additional Weight of Marginalized Stress and Microaggressions Resulting from Societal Privilege

Even though the male label is associated with assumed power and privilege, the reality of that power and privilege depends on how that sex label intersects with a person's identity, including their true gender identity, sexuality, racial or ethnic identity, religion, immigration status, socioeconomic status, or level of education.

You might not just carry the weight of a Ten-Ton Trauma; because of societal privilege enjoyed by others, you might also have the additional weight of marginalized stress and microaggressions.

Privilege

We live in a society of privileges: white privilege, cisgender privilege, heterosexual privilege, able-bodied privilege, and the list goes on.

White Privilege

White privilege means that someone who is White does not have to endure the overt or covert discrimination that is experienced by a person who is Black, Indigenous, or a Person of Color. Examples include:

- You do not have to fear being denied work because you are White.
- You do not have to fear being denied a home because you are White.
- You do not have to fear being denied a place of worship because you are White.
- You do not have to fear being denied the support of friends and family because you are White.
- You do not have to fear being denied your own personal safety, and the safety of your family, because you are White.
- There are role models in the media and in the political arena who are White.

Cisgender Privilege

If someone is given the male sex label at (or before) birth, and their true gender identity is in line with that, they are usually labeled cisgender.

As society is set up to assume (incorrectly) that people are cisgender, and assume (incorrectly) that being cisgender is the norm, someone who is cisgender benefits from the privilege of not having to endure the overt or covert discrimination that is experienced by a person who is transgender, non-binary, gender queer, two spirit, bigender, gender diverse, or any other gender identity that is not cisgender.

Examples of cisgender privilege include:

- You do not have to fear being denied the support of friends and family because of your true gender identity.
- You do not have to fear being denied your own personal safety, and the safety of your family, because of your true gender identity.
- You do not have to remind people (even your loved ones) of your pronouns, or your name (so you are not dead-named).
- You fill out a form and it asks you to tick the box "Male" or "Female."
- There are only two bathrooms, one labeled "Men" and one labeled "Women."
- You do not have to fear being denied work because of your true gender identity.

Heterosexual Privilege
Heterosexual privilege means that someone who is heterosexual does not have to endure the overt or covert discrimination that is experienced by someone who is bisexual, gay, pansexual, asexual, queer, or any other sexuality other than heterosexual.

Examples of heterosexual privilege include:

- You do not have to fear being denied work because of your sexuality.
- You do not have to fear being denied a home because of your sexuality.
- You do not have to fear being denied the support of friends and family because of your sexuality.
- You do not have to fear being denied your own personal safety, and the safety of your family, because of your sexuality.
- There are role models in the media and in the political arena who are heterosexual.

300

- There are rites of passage, public ceremonies, and other traditions based around the assumption of a heterosexual relationship.

Mental Workout Routine

Are you aware of any of these privileges in your own life? Have you benefited from any of them? Or have others benefited at your expense?

Use the space set out below to make a note of one example of White privilege, cisgender privilege, and heterosexual privilege.

1. Example of White privilege that has benefited you, or benefited others at your expense

```
                                                        
```

2. Example of cisgender privilege that has benefited you, or benefited others at your expense

```
                                                        
```

3. Example of heterosexual privilege that has benefited you, or benefited others at your expense

```
                                                        
```

Marginalized Stress

When society is set up to cater to, and benefit, the privileged, the result for other people can sometimes be devastating. One way to quantify this is to weigh up the additional weight of marginalized stress.

The "minority stress model" was introduced by I.H. Meyer, Senior Scholar for Public Policy at The Williams Institute, UCLA School of Law. Minority stress is stress caused by society discriminating against, inflicting violence on, and rejecting people who do not benefit from the various privileges. In addition, minority stress is also caused by the anticipation of this discrimination, or the acceptance of society's negative views (in the form of internalized phobias, such as internalized racism, internalized transphobia, internalized biphobia, and internalized homophobia).

Some argue that the term "minority" glosses over the fact that those targeted are *marginalized*, and they are not necessarily the minority. As a result, I will continue to refer to "marginalized stress," rather than "minority stress."

Researchers Edward Alessi and James Martin have shown that living with discrimination (for example, in the form of verbal or physical abuse, or structural oppression) creates symptoms similar to PTSD. Their study applied to members of the LGBTQ+ community, but it is easy to see how this can apply to many other marginalized groups, including

- a person who is Black, Indigenous, or a Person of Color;
- a person who is transgender, non-binary, gender queer, two spirit, bigender, gender diverse, or any other gender identity that is not cisgender, or;
- a person who is bisexual, gay, pansexual, asexual, queer, or any other sexuality other than heterosexual.

Marginalized stress is when someone experiences significantly higher levels of

- external discrimination (for example, harassment, verbal assaults, and alienation);

- the expectation of stressful events or discrimination (for example, hypervigilance, continuously assessing social events for potential attacks);
- internalized prejudice (the adoption of society's negative attitudes as your own views) in the form of internalized racism, internalized transphobia, internalized biphobia, and internalized homophobia.

Mental Workout Routine

Are you aware of any marginalized stress in your own life? If you have not carried the additional weight of marginalized stress yourself, do you know someone who has?

Use the space set out below to make a note of three examples of marginalized stress that you have experienced, or that you have witnessed in someone else.

1. Example of marginalized stress you have endured or witnessed

2. Example of marginalized stress you have endured or witnessed

3. Example of marginalized stress you have endured or witnessed

Microaggressions

Microaggressions are comments that communicate hostility, whether intentional or not, to target a person based solely upon their membership of a marginalized group. This is a concept introduced by Derald Wing Sue, Professor of Psychology and Education in the Department of Counseling and Clinical Psychology at Columbia University.

Here are some examples:

Example micro-aggressions against someone who is Black	Example micro-aggressions against someone who is Bisexual	Example micro-aggressions against someone who is Transgender
"I don't see color"	"Pick a side; are you gay or straight?"	"Are you a man or woman?"
"You are pretty skinny for a Black dude."	"You don't have to flaunt it in here."	"What is your real name?"

Figure 39 - Examples of Microaggressions

Mental Workout Routine

Are you aware of any microaggressions in your own life? If you have not carried the additional weight of microaggressions yourself, do you know someone who has?

Use the space set out below to make a note of three examples of microaggressions that you have experienced, or that you have witnessed in someone else.

1. *Example of microaggressions you have endured or witnessed*

| |
| |

2. *Example of microaggressions you have endured or witnessed*

| |
| |

3. *Example of microaggressions you have endured or witnessed*

| |
| |

* * *

As the male labeled are less likely to access mental healthcare, they are also less likely to get the help they need (even if they do seek help). If trauma, marginalized stress and microaggressions are left unchecked, it is a less safe, and less healthy society for all. So let's look at how to get beyond the blue of your Ten-Ton Trauma.

* * *

How to Escape the Weight of the Ten-Ton Trauma

Trauma is difficult to manage without the help of a trained professional, and so I have set out below some of the different forms of help available. In the next chapter, I will outline how you can find the help of a trained professional.

In their book *Trauma & Recovery*, Judith Herman sets out a three-stage process to escape the weight of the Ten-Ton Trauma.

1. Establish Safety

Safety means an ability to distinguish the past from the present. You are able to see that you are not stuck under the weight of the Ten-Ton Trauma, and this can be achieved using any of the grounding exercises set out later in this chapter.

2. Retell or Remember Your Trauma Story

Retelling or remembering your trauma story is important because the memory of trauma is often stored in fragmented ways. Unlike other stories of your past that have a beginning, a middle, and an end, trauma stories are stored like shards of glass, fragments of images, sounds, smells, and emotions.

By retelling or remembering your trauma story, you again feel in control of your life. You decide what to tell, how much, and when. With this new sense of power and control, you can rid yourself of the toxicity of terror, overwhelm, and shame, and you can achieve *integration,* where the trauma story has a beginning, a middle, and, most importantly, an end: you survived, and you are safe now.

Retelling your trauma story also helps with the integration needed between your limbic system and your prefrontal cortex. Instead of flipping our lid (as shown in Figure 38), you do the opposite and integrate the limbic system and your prefrontal cortex (as shown in Figure 37). As a result, you think more clearly.

Example
After Joseph was raped, they needed help in these ways:

When Joseph first saw a therapist, they refused to talk. They kept their guard up by leaving sessions early and refusing to answer any of the therapist's questions.

The therapist communicated respect for Joseph's pace, and they went slowly and gently, exploring all sorts of unrelated issues, including the lack of trash collection in Joseph's neighborhood, and the proliferation of bubble-tea shops at their local mall.

Eventually Joseph started to feel safe in therapy, and so they felt willing to tell their story of the rape. Part of that storytelling included an account of the emotions they experienced back then, and the emotions they felt in the present.

Initially Joseph was only aware of a head-pounding tightness all over their neck and shoulders, but eventually the therapist helped Joseph to become familiar with the entire spectrum of words available in their Flashlight. As a result, Joseph could identify each emotion as anger, loss, and hurt.

Joseph also needed to feel the full extent of their anger, loss, and hurt. Initially, Joseph tried to distract themself by working late, but one night Joseph broke down over the loss of their innocence, and the loss of trust in others. This hit Joseph in multiple waves of anger and pain.

Once Joseph could identify and feel these emotions, Joseph could grieve the loss of their innocence and trust in others.

The storytelling gave Joseph a newfound sense of control over the process, and so there was a consequential integration of their limbic system and prefrontal cortex. As a result, Joseph could think more clearly, and assess the present situation in terms of real, rather than imagined, threats.

Only after Joseph had told their story of the trauma, fully grieved for their losses, and integrated their limbic system with their prefrontal cortex, could they start to rebuild a sense of how to trust, and feel safe around, certain people in certain situations.

It is this part, a restored connection with your community, that we will turn to next.

But first, let's take a break.

Mental Workout Routine

Reading about trauma can be heavy going, so for five or ten minutes, take a breather in any way you need to. This could be one of the following suggestions, or something you choose.

- *Go for a walk around the block*
- *Engage in some light exercise*
- *Talk to a friend*
- *Watch something that makes you smile or laugh*
- *Meditate*
- *Do some stretching, whether it is some formal yoga or Pilates, or informal wriggling your limbs around*

3. Restore Connection with your Community

The third and final part of Judith Herman's approach to escaping the weight of the Ten-Ton Trauma involves a reconnection with your community. Trauma often involves a misuse of power, or a betrayal of trust, and so this can be a very difficult and precarious step to take. Why trust when you have had that trust ripped apart in the past?

Many strategies set out in Chapter 4 can help with this stage of your healing. Review that chapter if you need a reminder of those strategies because human connection is important.

The Superpower of Neuroplasticity

Remember when you went to camp and you dug deep into your backpack, only to find a Tootsie Roll you had forgotten from the week before? Well, if you dig deep into the backpack you are carrying along life's journey, you might just find your superpower called neuroplasticity.

You can literally create new neural pathways and teach your brain that life is not unsafe, that some people can be trusted, and we are not to blame.

Each safe, supportive, and rewarding experience you have, on your own or with your travel companions, can teach you that there are other ways to live beyond the fight-or-flight state.

Yes, your caregivers were assholes, and yes, you experienced violence with your first partner, and you never thought you would escape either situation, but you did. When you re-establish your safety, tell your trauma story, and reconnect with the safer travel companions along your journey, your brain can learn new tricks.

As much as you learned from your caregivers that the world is an unsafe place, and you cannot trust others to love and support you, you can unlearn all of this. I know many survivors of childhood trauma who do not just survive, they thrive at work and at home.

This brain of yours has helped you survive so far, so it is likely that it has numerous tricks and coping strategies that will continue to help you. One such trick or coping strategy is to make use of the Polyvagal Theory, and we will turn to that next.

Polyvagal Theory

Throughout this chapter we have been referring to the fight-or-flight state that we can get stuck in as a result of trauma. This is your sympathetic nervous system, or the green "Go Signal."

> *If you feel safe,* the sympathetic nervous system allows you to heed the Go Signal and become alert to perform — you can engage in sport, artwork, or even sex (*Wahoo, science finally gets exciting!*).

> *If you feel unsafe,* your sympathetic nervous system allows you to heed the Go Signal and you get ready to fight or flee.

With the sympathetic nervous system heeding the Go Signal, adrenaline is released, your blood pressure increases, your heart rate increases, and blood is sent to your limbs. If your sympathetic nervous system is constantly in a state of alertness, without a chance to calm and rest, your body can become depleted. As we have seen previously, this can have a significant impact on your physical health in terms of arthritis, heart disease, diabetes, and lung cancer.

Polyvagal Theory, as proposed by psychiatrist Stephen Porges, encourages us to make use of the opposite nervous system to our sympathetic nervous system, our parasympathetic nervous system. This is your "Stop Sign of Shut Down."

If you feel safe, your parasympathetic nervous system allows you to heed the Stop Sign of Shut Down by resting, sleeping, and meditating.

If you feel unsafe, your parasympathetic nervous system heeds the Stop Sign of Shut Down by freezing or dissociating.

Stephen Porges identifies two parts of the parasympathetic nervous system, and research indicates they offer two different responses to stress:

The Dorsal Vagal Nerve Network — In response to cues of a threat to your life, this is when your body and mind shuts down or dissociates. This happens when you cannot resolve something through social connection, and you cannot fight or flee.

The Ventral Vagal Nerve Network — In response to cues of safety, this is your social engagement system, and you activate it by engaging in human connection. In turn, you trigger calmness, and you reduce the levels of cortisol in your body (the stress hormone).

The Mighty Shield of Polyvagal Theory

If you want to put yourself into a calmer state to flex your superpower of neuroplasticity, you need to find as many ways as possible to activate your ventral vagal nerve network (your social engagement system.

Here are some suggestions:

- Try activities that engage the parts of the body where the ventral vagal nerve runs (anywhere from the diaphragm up to the brain stem), such as
  - breathing

311

- exercise
- singing and humming
- smiling and eye contact

• Connect more with your travel companions. We have already seen the benefit of the right kind of human connection. The most important components to this connection include compassion, trust, and a feeling of safety.

• Distract yourself from any stress-inducing thought processes by engaging all your senses. Later in this chapter. I will show you how to do this (using a grounding exercise).

• Do some vocal toning, which can be as simple as a simple sigh, or an affirming "*Ah, ha*" when you listen to someone.

Mental Workout Routine

Try a little vocal toning for yourself.

Breathe in for three seconds, and then breathe out for six seconds. As you breathe out, make some sort of audible sound such as "Aaaah" or "Ooooh," or even an Austin Powers, "Yeah, Baby!"
Make sure you breathe into the diaphragm, which is below your lungs.

Repeat the exercise several times, and notice how your mind and body starts to calm after each outward breath and audible sound.

Use the space set out below to make a note of what you notice before, during, and after you engage in some vocal toning.

1. What I notice before vocal toning

2. What I notice during vocal toning

3. What I notice after vocal toning

Familiarize Yourself with Your Nervous System

You will see from (Figure 40) why some people refer to the nervous system as a "flowchart" or "ladder" with
- the ventral vagal nerve network at the top;
- the sympathetic nervous system in the middle; and
- the dorsal vagal nerve network at the bottom.

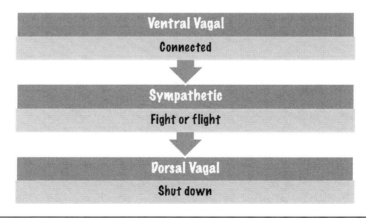

Figure 40 - Your Nervous System

Mental Workout Routine

Using the space below, familiarize yourself with your own nervous system by making a note of your experiences in
- *the ventral vagal zone (or "state");*
- *a sympathetic state; and*
- *the dorsal vagal zone (or "state").*

How to Recognize When You Are In a Particular Zone

This might help you to recognize when you are in a particular zone:

The ventral vagal zone — This is when you have felt curious, content, playful, or joyous.

A sympathetic state — This is when you have felt panicked, overwhelmed, angry, afraid, or felt like you wanted to fight or run away.

The dorsal vagal zone — This is when you have felt numb, disconnected, or shut down

For each of the three states, make a note of your typical experiences, namely:
- *The typical things you do (action or behavior)*
- *The typical things you think about (thoughts, including beliefs and assumptions),*
- *The typical emotions you feel*

Your typical experiences when you have been in the **ventral vagal zone.** *This is when you have felt curious, content, playful, or joyous (remember, this is the social engagement system):*

The typical things you do (action or behavior)

The typical things you think (thoughts, including beliefs and assumptions)

The typical emotions you feel

Your typical experiences when you have been in the **sympathetic state**. *This is when you have felt panicked, overwhelmed, angry, afraid, or felt like you wanted to fight or run away (remember, this includes the fight-or-flight state):*

The typical things you do (action or behavior)

The typical things you think (thoughts, including beliefs and assumptions)

The typical emotions you feel

Your typical experiences when you have been in the **dorsal vagal zone**. *This is when you have felt numb, disconnected, or shut down (remember, this includes the state of dissociation):*

The typical things you do (action or behavior)

The typical things you think (thoughts, including beliefs and assumptions)

The typical emotions you feel

State Shift, Perspective Shift?

Some say that the zone or state you are in (ventral, sympathetic, or dorsal, not New York or New Jersey) determines how you view yourself, your travel companions, and the world around you.

Mental Workout Routine

Using the space set out below, complete the sentences from the perspective of each of the three following states/zones:
- *the ventral vagal zone*
- *a sympathetic state*
- *the dorsal vagal zone*

*From the typical experiences you noted above, when you are in the **ventral vagal zone** (when you feel curious, content, playful, or joyous), complete each of the following sentences:*

I view myself as

I view my travel companions as

I view the world as

*From the Typical Experiences you noted above, when you are in the **sympathetic state** (when you have felt panicked, overwhelmed, angry, afraid, or you have felt like you wanted to fight or run away from the situation), complete each of the following sentences: -*

I view myself as

I view my travel companions as

I view the world as

*From the typical experiences you noted above, when you are in the **dorsal vagal zone** (when you have felt numb, disconnected, or shut down), complete each of the following sentences:*

I view myself as

I view my travel companions as

I view the world as

Mental Workout Routine

Time to take another break. For five or ten minutes, allow yourself to take a breather in any way you need to. This could be one of the following suggestions, or something you choose:

- *Go for a walk around the block*
- *Engage in some light exercise*
- *Talk to a friend*
- *Watch something that makes you smile or laugh*
- *Meditate*
- *Do some stretching, whether it is some formal yoga or Pilates, or informal wriggling your limbs around*

Eye Movement Desensitization and Reprocessing Therapy (EMDR)

Every working day in my psychotherapy practice I help people with the use of eye movement desensitization and reprocessing therapy (EMDR). You might have seen Prince Harry talking about it to Oprah, and I was overjoyed to see someone who is male labeled speaking out about psychotherapy, trauma, and EMDR. I hope this encourages more people who are male labeled to seek help, and get the right type of help.

The World Health Organization (WHO) considers EMDR to be an "A" level of treatment for trauma, and the National Institute for Clinical Excellence recognizes it as one of two empirically supported treatments of choice for adult PTSD.

EMDR helps you to let go of distressing memories that may be held in your body and mind. In turn, you are able to let go of unhelpful thoughts (such as *I am unsafe* or *I am out of control*). This frees your mind to find more adaptive ways to view the world (for example, *I have ways of keeping myself safe*, *I have tried my best,* or *I am now in control*).

Although you cannot administer EMDR yourself, you can use some of the concepts that are used in that approach. One such concept is the *Window of Tolerance*, and we will look at that next.

Escape through the Window of Tolerance

The Ten-Ton Trauma weighs heavily if you have no means of escape. It can crush the joy out of your life because you are stuck in the past, constantly flipping your lid over the small stuff.

Remember how stuck Charles felt, trapped in fear every time they heard the sound of footsteps on the stairs? Even though the original source of their torment, their abusive parent, died a decade ago, still Charles was trapped beneath the weight of a Ten-Ton Trauma, still stuck in the fight-or-flight response. Their reactions were neither proportionate to, nor appropriate for, present-day reality.

One means of escape from the ten-ton weight of trauma is through the Window of Tolerance. This is a small space in between the chaos where we can see, smell, hear, and breathe present-day reality. We are not hyperaroused (anxious, angry, agitated, and jumpy), and we are not hypoaroused (checked out, numb, as if our brain has left our body).

With the help of grounding exercises, we can create our own Window of Tolerance to respond to present-day situations in a proportionate and appropriate way. The more we are grounded in present-day reality, the less likely we are to remain trapped by the past, under the weight of this Ten-Ton Trauma.

Grounding Exercises

There are numerous grounding exercises out there, beyond the blue. Here are three for you to try.

1. Use Labels to Your Advantage

Mental Workout Routine

Finally, labels have a useful purpose. Use the labeled categories set out below to name as many items as possible within each category. For example, if you were to choose the animal category, you could list a dog, cat, donkey, snake, camel… and you get the idea.

- *Actors*
- *Animals*
- *Business People*
- *Cities*
- *Colors*
- *Countries*
- *Drinks*
- *Foods*
- *Singers*

For 3 bonus points - Award yourself 3 bonus points if you manage to engage in this exercise at least once a week within the next three weeks.

Subtotal of bonus points so far: _____

2. Five, Four, Three, Two, and One

Mental Workout Routine

If the weight of your Ten-Ton Trauma has kept you stuck in the past, you can help your mind to realize that you are safe in the present. Do this by using a similar Mental Workout Routine that you saw in Chapter 2.

Use all your senses to notice your surroundings, and by the time you get to one taste, you should be grounded in the present moment.

1. Notice and describe to yourself five things you can see. Notice the colors, textures, shapes, and shadows.
2. Notice and describe to yourself four things that you can touch. Go on and run your hands over them, and notice the smooth or roughness, the bumpiness, the heat or coolness of each item.
3. Notice and describe to yourself three things that you can hear. Notice the loudness or softness of each

sound, and allow the sound to reverberate around your ears. How does it feel to hear each sound?

4. Notice and describe to yourself two things that you can smell. What is it like to smell each of these? And what do each of these smells evoke in you?

5. Notice and describe to yourself one thing that you can taste. Savor the taste, and just let it rest in your mouth for a little. What is that like?

For 3 bonus points - Award yourself 3 bonus points if you manage to engage in this exercise at least once a week within the next three weeks.

Subtotal of bonus points so far: _____

3. Use Your Body as an Anchor

Mental Workout Routine

You can ground yourself in the present moment by using your body as an anchor. Earlier in this Survival Guide you saw how you can use your breathing apparatus to do this, but there is more to your body than just your lungs.

1. Notice how it feels to make a physical connection between your body and your surroundings. For example, how does it feel with each foot placed firmly on the ground? Does one foot make more contact with the ground than the other? Does one part of your foot make more contact than another part? Is the ground hard or soft beneath your feet?

Adopt the same sense of curiosity to other parts of your body that might be making contact with your surroundings.

2. Clench and release each muscle group throughout your body. What is that like? Does it feel relaxing, or loosening? Does it waken you up a bit?

3. Tap your feet on the ground, and then your hands on your lap. What is that like? Does your lap feel warm or cool beneath your skin? Does it feel hard or soft?
4. Reach for the sky and stretch out your arms. Do you notice the blood flow changing ever so slightly? Does it make your mind feel a little more awake?
5. Pick up an object and feel it in your hands. It could be a cushion or a rock, or a pen, or a piece of fabric. Just notice every last texture under your skin.

For 3 bonus points - Award yourself 3 bonus points if you manage to engage in this exercise at least once a week within the next three weeks.

Subtotal of bonus points so far: _____

When you engage in any grounding exercise, pay special attention to each of the following points:

- **Your Thought Process** *(your beliefs and assumptions) — For example, you might initially assume this is not going to help you, or you assume it is not safe to engage in this exercise.*

- **Your Emotions** *— For example, you might be afraid of what this exercise might lead to, or you feel hopeless that nothing is going to help.*

- **Your Bodily Sensations** *— For example, you notice that your shoulders and neck are rigid. Pay particular attention to your body because your body acts as a bridge between your emotions and your conscious awareness. Your bodily sensations might tell you something important about what should change. If you want to learn more about this important bridge, read The Body Keeps the Score by Bessel van der Kolk.*

Mental Workout Routine

Use the space set out below to make a note of what you notice before, during, and after each grounding exercise.

- *When I engage in this Mental Workout Routine, I notice the following things about my **thought process** (my beliefs and assumptions):*

    Before

    During -

    After -

- *When I engage in this Mental Workout Routine, I notice the following things about my **emotions**:*

    Before

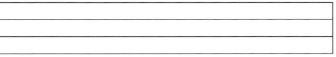

    During

After

- *When I engage in this Mental Workout Routine, I notice the following things about my **bodily sensations**:*

Before

During

After

* * *

Escape the Ten-Ton Trauma Using Your Survival Tools

Trapped under the weight of the Ten-Ton Trauma, you can get stuck in the same type of cycle that we have seen in the previous chapters -

- <u>Your Action Pack (behavior)</u> — Trapped under the weight of this Ten-Ton Trauma, you can end up doing less of the things that usually make you feel good. As a result, your Head Gear stops working so well.

- <u>Your Head Gear (thoughts)</u> — The less you do, the more negative your thoughts are. The lack of engagement with fulfilling things acts as proof that you really are not good enough. What makes matters worse, all of us have Head Gear that can develop the occasional fault, and when that happens, we are even less able to heave that weight of trauma from on top of us.

- <u>The Flashlight (emotions)</u> — The more negative or faulty your Head Gear, the worse you feel. Your emotions darken as you peer through gloomy eyes, and your Flashlight dims to a barely visible glow.

And so, the trauma cycle continues.

Figure 41 - The Trauma Cycle

But it doesn't have to be this way, and you can use your Survival Tools to break free of this vicious trauma cycle:

- Action Pack — Engage in actions that once made you feel good. This will give you new experiences to lift your thoughts.

- Your Head Gear — The less negative, and the less faulty, your thought process, the more likely your emotions will start to lift

- Your Flashlight — The more you can master the Dimmer Switch on that Flashlight and regulate your emotions, the easier you will find that dizzying dialectic of trauma

  When you feel too little – You can turn up the Dimmer Switch when you start to feel vacant in body and mind, and

  When you feel too much – You can turn down the Dimmer Switch when you feel it all, at every moment.

Shelter of Resilience

You will recall that we also have a Shelter of Resilience to keep you safe, when you need to rest from this journey. Review Chapter 1 if you need a reminder of how to construct it and its four walls.

* * *

If You Are in Crisis

Trauma is one of the hardest weights that anyone will have to bear. It is exceptionally difficult to manage this alone, so if you find yourself beyond the blue and think you are in crisis, seek immediate professional help. Please turn to Appendix Crisis for further information.

* * *

Survive and Thrive Recap

In this chapter, you

- learned how to identify a Ten-Ton Trauma;
- explored the myths surrounding trauma and the male label, including the intersection of the male label with your racial or ethnic identity, true gender identity, or sexuality;
- appreciated the additional weight of marginalized stress and microaggressions, as a result of societal privilege;
- learned that trauma is difficult to manage without the help of a trained professional, and so you learned about some of the different forms of help available, including –
  - o Judith Herman's three-stage process of establishing safety, retelling your trauma story, and reconnecting with your community,
  - o the superpower of neuroplasticity
  - o the mighty shield of Polyvagal Theory
  - o EMDR therapy, including concepts such as
    - an escape through the Window of Tolerance
    - the use of grounding exercises
  - o your Survival Tools
  - o your Shelter of Resilience.

We need to let our imagination go beyond the blue of the male label. If we can accept that the male labeled do suffer from trauma, and this might remain undetected because of misconceptions about the male label, and, in some cases, due to structural obstacles, we can give help to those who need it. This will lead to a safer and healthier society for all, before we are lost beyond the blue of trauma.

Beyond the Blue

CHAPTER 6

BEYOND THE BLUE OF BAD AND UGLY HELP

No matter how hard you try to get beyond the blue of your depression, anxiety, relationship conflict, or trauma, you might still need professional help. Here are some of the reasons why:

- You haven't the time to work it out on your own (you are probably getting eyestrain from the glare of your phone as you try to Google answers to these problems).
- Your friends or family do not have time to listen to you.
- Your friends or family listen, but they do not listen objectively.
- You feel guilty about burdening your friends or family.

More seriously, you might be in need of help because the level of your need surpasses the help that can be offered in this Survival Guide. This is why healthcare professionals were invented, and so here is a list of different ones you could approach:

- licensed professional counselors
- licensed clinical social workers
- psychotherapists
- psychiatrists
- psychologists.

Other professionals, such as primary care physicians or registered nurse practitioners, might have some knowledge about how to help you, but (unlike the above-mentioned professionals) mental health is not their primary area of expertise.

Whichever type of healthcare professional you choose to engage, you need to recognize what constitutes the good, the bad, and the downright ugly forms of help. You deserve a trained and experienced professional who can see beyond the blue of the male label, and beyond any preconceived notions that are tainted by racism, transphobia, biphobia, homophobia, or any other type of prejudice.

Separating the Good from the Bad and Ugly Forms of Help

Striving for accessible mental healthcare is all well and good, but what if you finally get to access the healthcare and it is far from adequate?

Do you recognize any of these signs of *Bad and Ugly Help*?

- The healthcare professional seems far from trained or professional.
- They smile and nod, but offer little in terms of insight or expertise.
- They are defensive when you challenge them.
- They make sweeping claims about the efficacy of their approach, without any sort of evidence.
- They make assumptions about you, your lifestyle, your preferences, and your problems,
- They use labels to make wild generalizations about you or anyone else.
- They can only see a binary concept of gender, referring to their clients, colleagues, and the rest of the world, as "he or she."

- They enquire about your wife when you have talked about your spouse or partner (choosing to ignore the fact that you may be bisexual, gay, or any sexuality other than heterosexual).
- They refer to "couples therapy" rather than "relationship therapy" (choosing to ignore the existence of any other intimate relationship; for example, polyamory).
- They are quick to take your money but slow to assume responsibility.
- They side with you (or against you) on every topic you raise.
- They have no interest in following through with promises, or following up with developments.
- They comment on your hairy chest with a smile and a smirk.
- They engage in any form of intimate or otherwise sexual behavior with you.
- There is any sort of dual relationship with you (in other words, they already know you in another setting, for example, as a friend, colleague, business associate, or family member).
- They pathologize you, quickly slapping a diagnostic label on you without much explanation or justification.
- They are unwilling to admit blind spots or a lack of knowledge.
- They take advantage of your working relationship with them (for example, they get from you the name of a recommended contractor).
- They act, directly or indirectly, in a way that demonstrates prejudice or a lack of cultural awareness, including (but not limited to) racism, transphobia, biphobia, or homophobia.
- They are unwilling to make a referral to a more appropriate healthcare professional.

Mental Workout Routine

Does any of this bring back bad memories?
If so, make a note of three examples of Bad and Ugly Help that you have received, or you have heard about from someone else

1.
2.
3.

Help That Takes You Beyond The Male label

As we saw in previous chapters, Bad and Ugly Help can result in further obstacles for the male labeled. This can have serious, potentially fatal consequences when it comes to depression, anxiety, relationship conflict, and trauma.

Here is a quick reminder of the Bad and Ugly Help when it comes to the male labeled.

- Some healthcare professionals do not recognize that the behavior of the male labeled (for example, anger and irritation) may be symptoms of the Beast of Depression, the Fireball of Anxiety, or the Ten-Ton Trauma.
- Some healthcare professionals believe in, and perpetuate, myths that the male labeled are somehow intrinsically unable to feel certain emotions, or they are intrinsically unable to suffer from depression, anxiety, and trauma.
- There is a higher rate of diagnosis of the male labeled when it comes to externalizing disorders such as ADD, oppositional defiant disorder,

conduct disorder, antisocial personality disorder, or substance-related disorders.

- The higher rate of diagnosis of these externalizing disorders is compounded when we consider a person's identity beyond the blue of their male label (for example, due to the racism, transphobia, biphobia, or homophobia of the diagnosing healthcare professionals).

Bad and Ugly Help Perpetuates Marginalized Stress and Microaggressions

Even though a healthcare professional claims to be a "helping professional," they can be far from helpful when they perpetuate marginalized stress and microaggressions.

Marginalized Stress

I have worked alongside healthcare professionals who have said things like –
"Isn't it nice that I don't see your color?"
"Boys will be boys"
"Isn't it great that your sexuality isn't an issue?"
"You are gay? Well, I hope you are practicing safe sex"
"Our job is to focus on you, not fix society's problems"

The same healthcare professionals refuse to accept that
- society is set up to cater to, and benefit the privileged, whether that privilege is White, cisgender, or heterosexual;
- mental and physical health is severely impacted by structural inequality;
- these professionals are living and breathing privilege, and yet many do not recognize their own.

Marginalized stress is caused and perpetuated by healthcare professionals like these.

Microaggressions

You may have spotted microaggressions in the examples of Bad and Ugly Help set out earlier in this chapter. Here is a quick recap of some of them:

- They make assumptions about you, your lifestyle, your preferences, and your problems.
- They use labels to make wild generalizations about you or anyone else.
- They can only see a binary concept of gender, referring to their clients, colleagues, and the rest of the world, as "he or she."
- They enquire about your wife when you have talked about your spouse or partner (choosing to ignore the fact that you might be bisexual, gay, or any other sexuality other than heterosexual).
- They refer to couples therapy rather than relationship therapy (choosing to ignore the existence of any other intimate relationship; for example, polyamory).
- They are unwilling to admit blind spots or lack of knowledge.
- They act, directly or indirectly, in a way that demonstrates prejudice or a lack of cultural awareness, including (but not limited to) racism, transphobia, biphobia, and homophobia.
- They are unwilling to make a referral to a more appropriate healthcare professional.

The Rot of Racism

If you are Black, Indigenous, or a Person of Color, I am sure you are well aware of racism. This section is more to help people who might not already recognize the *rot of racism*.

Here are just some of the signs that the Rot of Racism has set in:

1.   Perpetuation of White Privilege

If a healthcare professional believes that being White is somehow the *"norm"* or *"preferred "*racial or ethnic identity, they might end up pathologizing a person who is Black, Indigenous, or a Person of Color. A healthcare professional might also be unaware of their own White privilege, and even when they become aware, they might refuse to accept that it has a significant impact on their work as a healthcare professional.

2.   Microaggressions

A healthcare professional might make assumptions based on the fact that someone is Black, Indigenous, or a Person of Color, or they might confuse two different clients, both of whom happen to be Black, Indigenous, or a Person of Color.

Further examples of microaggressions are set out earlier in this Survival Guide.

The Transmutation of Transphobia

If you are transgender, non-binary, gender queer, two spirit, bigender, gender diverse, or any gender identity other than cisgender, I am sure you are well aware of transphobia. This section is more to help people who might not already recognize the *transmutation of transphobia*.

Here are some of the symptoms of the *transmutation of transphobia*:

1.   Perpetuation of the Gender Identity Myths

If a healthcare professional believes in the Gender Binary Myth or the Cisgender Myth, this is a sign that they have been *transmuted by transphobia.*

> **The Gender Binary Myth:** *Once upon a time, in a land far, far away, there lived a man and a woman, and no other gender identity ever existed.*
> This is known as the Gender Binary Myth, the mistaken belief that gender identity comprises two options: "man" or "woman". Linked to this is the (also mistaken) belief that gender identity is discoverable and fixed from birth, and a further mistaken belief that gender identity is the same as a sex label.
> The Gender Binary Myth is a product of certain societies (including the United States), but in other societies, and at other times in history, gender identity has been a matter of a spectrum, and it has not been fixed or discoverable at one point in time.
>
> Professional bodies such as the American Psychological Association (APA) have confirmed that "gender is a non-binary construct that allows for a range of gender identities" (APA Guidelines, 2015).
>
> **The Cisgender Myth (Cisgenderism):** This is the mistaken belief that the cisgender identity is in some way the "norm", or the "idealized" form of gender identity.

If a healthcare professional demonstrates that they believe in either Gender Identity Myth, they may end up pathologizing someone who is any gender identity other than cisgender. If they imply that being any gender identity other than cisgender is wrong, you should report them to their licensing state and governing body (for example, the

337

American Counseling Association, American Psychological Association, National Association of Social Workers, or the American Psychiatric Association).

2.   Confusion

If a healthcare professional has been transmuted by transphobia, they might confuse gender identity and sexuality. They might also confuse sex labels with gender identity.

3.   Microaggressions

Your healthcare professional might end up using microaggressions, and you have seen examples earlier on in this Survival Guide.

The Horror of Homophobia and Biphobia

If you are bisexual, gay, pansexual, asexual, queer, or any other sexuality that is not heterosexual, I am sure you are well aware of the signs of homophobia and biphobia. This section is more to help people who might not already recognize the horror of *homophobia and biphobia.*

Here are just some of the *horrors of homophobia and biphobia*.

1.   Perpetuation of Heteronormativity

If a healthcare professional believes that heterosexuality is somehow the "norm" or "preferred" sexuality, they may end up pathologizing someone who is bisexual, gay, pansexual, asexual, queer, or any other sexuality that is not heterosexual. This is a harmful practice, and it implies that any sexuality other than being heterosexual is a disease that needs to be cured. This practice should be reported to the professional's licensing state and governing body.

2. Confusion

One sure-fire symptom of the *horror of homophobia and biphobia* is to confuse gender identity and sexuality.

3. Microaggressions

Your professional might end up referring to someone's sexuality as a "phase." More examples of microaggressions are set out earlier in this Survival Guide.

Blind Help...Leading Us Further Off A Cliff?

When you seek shelter from depression, anxiety, relationship conflict or trauma, you should be particularly wary of a professional who claims to be blind to

- racial or ethnic identity;
- true gender identity; or
- sexuality.

Studies show that adopting a gender-blind, sexuality-blind, or color-blind approach is unhelpful. Here are a few reasons why.

1. Knowing you inside and out

To help you to survive depression, anxiety, relationship conflict or trauma, the healthcare professional needs to know everything about you (the male label you were given, but also your true gender identity, your sexuality, and your racial or ethnic identity), and how your experiences are informed by all of this.

All of this will have an impact on the challenges you face, but also the strengths and resources you can use to survive depression, anxiety, relationship conflict, or trauma. To adopt a blind approach, the healthcare professional will not see the whole of you.

2. Structural oppression

Depression, anxiety, relationship conflict, and trauma all thrive on racism, transphobia, homophobia, and biphobia. We can arrange all the therapy sessions in the world, but without changes to address these issues at a structural level, we are missing the point. A healthcare professional has a duty to tackle the depression, anxiety, relationship conflict, and trauma at a structural *and* an individual level. This is impossible if a healthcare professional adopts a blind approach.

3. The Additional Weight of Marginalized Stress and Microaggressions

If a healthcare professional ignores structural oppression, they will fail to understand the additional weight that many people have to carry due to marginalized stress and microaggressions, and the role that privilege plays in that.

Unicorns Need Not Apply

Every living and breathing healthcare professional will have their own cultural bias. They will make assumptions, they will have a certain amount of power and privilege (even if it is only in the form of their role as a healthcare professional), and they will have their own blind spots through a lack of personal or professional experience. So we are not looking for a unicorn.

We just need a healthcare professional who is aware of these biases and blind spots, and actively reflects on these by regularly checking them out. They can do this in the following ways:

- Talking to you, the client, about all of this (as long as they do not rely on you for their free cultural education)
- Reflecting on their biases and blind spots in their own professional supervision. This is where they discuss their clients, without disclosing identifying characteristics, with other healthcare professionals.
- They pursue their own ongoing personal therapy. Because of the danger of "*Nodding Dog Syndrome*" in supervision groups (where healthcare professionals end up just nodding in agreement with whatever happens to be the general consensus), it is my belief that healthcare professionals should be permanently engaged in their own personal therapy for life.

Remember that each healthcare professional should be licensed in the state where they practice (and the state where their client is receiving those services). Usually that license requires the professional to act in accordance with the Code of Ethics that applies to their profession.

If you have any doubts about your healthcare professional, particularly if they are racist, transphobic, biphobic, or homophobic, check the Code of Ethics for their professional organization and raise a complaint with the licensing board in the state they are licensed.

Good Help Beyond Diagnostic Labels

You deserve help that takes you beyond your labels, and sometimes that means help beyond any diagnostic label. I mentioned in the Introduction that I have heard healthcare professionals referring to people as *problematic borderlines, bipolars,* or *narcissists* without any attempt to understand that person's needs, or how much they might have suffered before they set foot in the professional's office. Too often mere lip service is paid to any Ten-Ton Trauma the person may be carrying, or the Beast of Depression that causes them to snap and snarl.

As we've seen, the very subject of a diagnosis is not without controversy. It is far from certain where one diagnosis begins and another ends, so the very diagnostic label can be questionable. And the adequacy of the "help" that is offered becomes a secondary question to the need to slap a diagnostic label on the person, as if that will somehow be the beginning and end to *Good Help.*

Good Help should involve the healthcare professional's discussion with you about the following:
- The appropriateness of a diagnostic label
- The appropriateness of the treatment
- The adequacy of how the treatment is applied (that is, the competence of the professional)

As we've seen, there is value in sometimes looking beyond the restrictive nature of a diagnostic label for depression, anxiety, and trauma. Whether or not you want your professional to do the same is your call, and there might be good reasons why they lean towards such a label (for example, to secure funding for your treatment). Good Help should include an open dialogue about this, without any assumption that the healthcare professional holds the deciding vote.

Good Help Beyond Dependence

Your healthcare professional needs time to get to know you, so from the outset, you are the expert of you. They will need to work hard to learn about you, so avoid any healthcare professional who

- talks over you;
- assumes anything about you;
- claims to have all the answers; or
- seems unwilling to hear your feedback.

No one has the miracle cure for depression, anxiety, relationship conflict, or trauma. Sorry to burst that bubble. But a healthcare professional should work hard to help you to understand more about you, and see where you might have overlooked a few areas of your process.

A good healthcare professional should help you to see and hear things about yourself, so you can use that knowledge to make better choices about your life. As you start to process this new insight, they can offer theories that may or may not resonate with you, including new developments from neuroscience, psychology, and other fields of research. But even these professionals are fallible people, with their own areas of focus, and their own prejudices. Remember that when it comes to many professionals, they are glorified mirror-holders; their job is to help you see yourself without distortion. Don't let them get too caught up in their own image where they end up flipping the mirror away from you.

Fifteen Steps to Good Help

Your healthcare professional should help you to do fifteen things. If they are any good, your professional will welcome you reviewing this checklist with them.

1. Use a Strengths-Based Approach – Your healthcare professional should help you to identify your strengths, and they should acknowledge that the male labeled is a diverse group of individuals. As a result, that professional should appreciate how hard it might have been to get to them in the

first place, and they should think carefully about how they may need to tailor their services to suit your unique needs. This stands in sharp contrast to a deficit-based approach, which only points out what is "wrong" with you, and how you are not fitting within a preconceived notion of how you "should" be, and what help is available to address that "deficit."

2.   Give you a rough indication of the length of the helping arrangement (including a regular review of this timescale).

3.   Set goals to work towards.

4.   Help you to address these seemingly contradictory desires:
- We have a desire for change, but
- We also have a desire for stability

5.   Help you to meet your needs, working up through what is known as Maslow's Hierarchy of Needs. This was created by psychologist Abraham Maslow, and it summarizes human needs into a hierarchy of priority:
- Physiological needs (food, water, warmth, rest)
- Safety needs (security, safety)
- Belongingness and love needs (intimate relationships, friendships)
- Esteem needs (prestige, and a sense of accomplishment)
- Self-actualization (achieve your full potential, including creative activity).

6.   Help you to identify and use a SMART Action Pack (behavior).

7. Help you to identify and challenge any faults in your Head Gear (thoughts, including beliefs and assumptions).

8. Help you to master your Flashlight (emotions), including your Dimmer Switch.

9. Help you to clarify how you view yourself, and how you view others.

10. Help you to see how you compensate for any perceived insecurities

11. Reflect on helpful and unhelpful ways you resolve problems in life.

12. Search for examples of competency and mastery.

13. Create new opportunities for competency and mastery.

14. Psycho-educate you (for example, you can learn more about your nervous system so you can understand why you feel a certain way in certain situations).

15. Enhance your motivation.

Where You Can Find Good Help

	A Talking Professional	A Medicating Professional	A Triaging Professional
Job Title	Psychotherapist, Counselor, Clinical Social Worker, Psychologist	Psychiatrist, Registered Nurse Practitioner	Primary Care Physician (PCP), Physician at Emergency Room of Hospital, or Urgent Care facility
How to Find Them	Recommendations from your insurance company, or your PCP. Online reviews	Recommendations from your insurance company, or your PCP. Online reviews	Recommendations from your insurance company, or your PCP. Online reviews

Figure 42 - How to Find Good Help

If You Are in Crisis

If you find yourself beyond the blue and you think you are in crisis, seek immediate professional help. Please turn to Appendix Crisis for further information.

* * *

Survive and Thrive Recap

In this chapter, you learned how to separate the Good from the Bad and Ugly forms of professional help, paying particular attention to

- Good Help that takes you beyond the male label;
- Bad and Ugly Help that perpetuates marginalized stress and microaggressions; and

- Fifteen Steps to Good Help.

If the male labeled can get Good Help that sees beyond the male label, without perpetuating marginalized stress or microaggressions, we might take a step closer to a safer and healthier society for all, before we are lost beyond the blue of Bad and Ugly Help.

CONCLUSION

A FORK IN THE ROAD, BUT NOT THE END OF OUR JOURNEY

Life's journey is a wilderness, but as we reach this fork in the road, you are in a better position to survive and thrive in spite of the following threats to your well-being:

- Depression snarling over your shoulder like a Beast
- Anxiety burning through the pit of your stomach like a Fireball
- Conflict and anger when it comes to the people who accompany you through life's wilderness
- Ten-Tons of Trauma crushing down on you.

These potential pitfalls are much less likely to threaten your career, your business, your education, or any personal relationships, given:

> You know how to use three Survival Tools to break free of the cycles of depression, anxiety, anger, and trauma –
> - Your Action Pack (your behavior)
> - Your Head Gear (your thought process, including your beliefs and assumptions)
> - Your Flashlight (your emotions).
>
> You also know how to construct and maintain the Four Walls of your Shelter of Resilience –
> - Self-Compassion
> - Self-Esteem
> - Self-Awareness through Acceptance
> - Self-Care.

You have learned about the benefit of human connection, and you identified the elements of the right kind of human connection, including
- a healthy balance, free of distortions, and free of abuse in all its forms (physical, emotional, financial, and isolation),
- trust;
- secure attachment; and
- assertiveness, including assertive communication of all emotions, including anger.

You understand that trauma is difficult to manage without the help of a trained professional, and you learned about some of the different forms of help available, including
- Judith Herman's three-stage process (establishing safety, retelling your trauma story, and reconnecting with your community)
- the superpower of neuroplasticity
- the mighty shield of the Polyvagal Theory
- eye movement desensitization and reprocessing therapy (EMDR).

If you do need the help of a trained professional, you learned how to separate the Good from the Bad and Ugly forms of help.

As you continue your journey through the wilderness that is your life, you will no doubt encounter further challenges, and it is my hope that you will continue to use this Survival Guide to survive but also to thrive.

Our journey together does not have to end. Our paths may coincide in the future in the following ways:

- You might need to clarify things that were raised in this Survival Guide
- You might need another survival guide for one or more of the following topics -
  o Perfectionism
  o Procrastination
  o Obsessions
  o Grief
  o Familial estrangement
  o Parenting
  o Workplace conflict
  o Violence
  o Substance misuse
- You might need a survival guide for a friend or family member, to help them better understand some of the issues that you face.
- You might need a survival guide for a professional who needs further information about any of the issues that have arisen in our journey together (that professional might be someone who works in a healthcare setting, in human resources, in a school, in a university, or in a religious organization).

In any of these circumstances, you are welcome to get in contact via the Contact page at www.chriswarrendickins.com

* * *

Blue is the color that represents the male label, and in patriarchal societies such as the United States the male label is associated with assumed power and privilege. The reality of that power and privilege is far more complicated, especially when it comes to depression, anxiety, relationship conflict, and trauma.

Any instances of untreated mental health issues leaves a society less safe and healthy for all. And yet societal conditioning related to the male label makes seeking help for depression, anxiety, relationship conflict, and trauma complicated, and this is compounded when the male label intersects with a person's true gender identity, their sexuality, or their racial or ethnic identity (for example, there are structural barriers to accessible mental healthcare, and there is racism, transphobia, biphobia, and homophobia).

No matter how much we attempt to fix the faults in our Head Gear, or master the Dimmer Switch on our Flashlight, we will not achieve a safer, healthier society without structural reform.

In this Black Swan Song, make it your mission to:

1. In any given context, monitor any privilege that is attached to the male label
2. Discover who might carry an additional burden as a result of that privilege
3. Weigh up any additional weight someone has to carry as a result of marginalized stress or microaggressions
4. Identify three SMART Actions you will take to address structural reform

I wish you luck as you continue your journey *Beyond the Blue*.

APPENDIX CRISIS

IF YOU ARE IN CRISIS

If you find yourself beyond the blue, and your depression, anxiety, relationship conflict, or trauma is about to make you do something harmful, you are in crisis and you must seek immediate, professional help.

Here is a reminder of some of the ways to seek immediate professional help:

- Call 911 (if it is available in your area)
- Take yourself to the Emergency Room of your nearest hospital
- Call a friend or family member, and ask them to take you to the nearest Emergency Room
- Call the National Suicide Helpline on 800-273-8255 / www.suicidepreventionlifeline.org

Know that when you are in crisis, your brain is less likely to function to its greatest ability. This means that you might only consider a limited list of options when in reality there might be many more ways to resolve your problems. This means you should seek help and ensure a trained and experienced professional is there to ensure your safety, and help you get out of your current state of crisis.

ABOUT THE AUTHOR

Figure 43 - Chris Warren-Dickins LLB MA LPC.
Photo credit: Jean Terman Photography

Chris Warren-Dickins is a psychotherapist, and they provide a psychotherapy service that serves people in New Jersey (USA) and the United Kingdom. Chris loves to help all sorts of people with all kinds of problems, and they tend to work on the following areas: Eye movement desensitization and reprocessing therapy (EMDR) (an approach commonly used for trauma), Affirmative LGBTQ+ therapy, and *"Men's therapy"* (in other words, *how to survive the male label*).

Chris was educated at University College London and University of East London (United Kingdom), and in 2010 Chris was awarded a Masters in Counseling & Psychotherapy. This included qualitative research into male-labeled experiences of suicide and counseling.

Before qualifying as a psychotherapist, Chris was a senior lawyer in London (United Kingdom), but Chris realized that they preferred to help people to feel safe and valued.

After building a successful psychotherapy practice in London (United Kingdom), Chris moved to the United States, to enable their two children to see more of their American grandparents, cousins, and wider family. Since 2018, Chris has been running a private psychotherapy practice in Ridgewood, New Jersey as a Licensed Professional Counselor (LPC).

Chris would love it if you reached out and made contact. Please do so via the Contact page at
www.chriswarrendickins.com.

THANK YOU / BONUS MATERIAL

By hook or by crook, you managed to get your hands on this Survival Guide. This shows that you have a determination that needs to be rewarded. Use the following link to get your Bonus Material -

http://eepurl.com/gD41jr

ADDITIONAL BONUS

At the start of our journey together, I mentioned that I would reward you with an Additional Bonus if you scored more than 50 bonus points in the Mental Workout Routines. Please use the following link to get your Additional Bonus -

https://mailchi.mp/a54778ab97b9/additionalbonus

INDEX